"*Faithful Leaders* focuses on two of the most neglected yet most crucial dimensions of leadership: character and godliness. In the plethora of 'how to' books, this book offers a compass—or a lifeline—to active Christians struggling with discouragement and defeat."

J.D. GREEAR, President, the Southern Baptist Convention;
Pastor, The Summit Church, Raleigh/Durham, North Carolina

"There is a crisis of confidence in leadership in our culture because so many in authority have failed to act with integrity and honesty. Tragically this has been replicated in the church as once-respected leaders have too often been revealed to be false teachers, hypocrites, abusers or self-servers. This book is a timely warning and encouragement to pastors and other church leaders to guard their hearts against sin so that they serve Christ and his people faithfully. Rico writes with clarity, honesty and personal vulnerability as he opens and applies the Scriptures. This powerful word is just what we need to hear."

JOHN STEVENS, National Director, FIEC

"This book is timely, realistic, honest, searching and relentlessly biblical. Above all, I found it searingly challenging in a way which moved me to take action in my own life. We don't just need to read *Faithful Leaders* but to live it."

GARY MILLAR, Principal, Queensland Training College,
Australia; Author, *Need to Know*

"I suspect many of us, not just church leaders, spend too much time chasing after success in the eyes of the world (whatever that might be) instead of pursuing faithfulness in the eyes of the Lord. This book is a helpful and much needed corrective."

CARRIE SANDOM, Director of Women's Ministry,
The Proclamation Trust

"Rico Tice has provided ministry leaders with a gem here. There are many books on leadership today, but many ignore or give little consideration to the overwhelming emphases in Scripture, and Tice helps us prioritize these biblical values. I will be using it in classes and training programs in the days ahead."

TONY MERIDA, Pastor for Preaching and Vision, Imago Dei Church, Raleigh, North Carolina; Director of Theological Training for Acts 29

"*Faithful Leaders* is a joy to read. Full of wisdom and focused on themes that leadership books ought to be about (but often aren't), it is somehow both challenging and encouraging at the same time. Reading it made me reflect, and write notes in my Bible, and pray. Wonderfully done."

ANDREW WILSON, Teaching Pastor, King's Church London

"I could easily have assumed that this was written for those younger in church leadership—but then I discovered it was written for me in my third decade in ministry. Time, tiredness and the sheer toughness of pastoral ministry take their toll, and it is so easy to drift into self-pity, self-indulgence and self-deception. Read this book honestly, and you will be humbled and, yes, frightened. I was. But you will be helped, and your ministry will perhaps be saved from eternal regret, for eternal reward."

WILLIAM J.U. PHILIP, Senior Minister, The Tron Church, Glasgow

"As go the shepherds, so go the sheep. Consequently, it's vital for ministry leaders to understand not just where to lead God's people but also how to lead God's people. The message of this book is one that every Christian leader needs to be reminded of over and again. Whether you are a young or an older leader, a new or experienced leader, pick up this book to remind yourself that it's not what people say about you and your ministry that matters. Ultimately, we seek the approval of our Lord."

JUAN R. SANCHEZ, Senior Pastor, High Pointe Baptist Church, Austin, Texas; Author, *7 Dangers Facing Your Church*

"In *Faithful Leaders* Rico Tice raises his voice to urge us to refocus our ambitions on what matters most. He does so with his characteristic passion for Christ and sobering directness. But he also writes as a humble fellow pilgrim, not as one who has arrived without a struggle. The author comes on his knees to serve us and to urge us to 'strive … for the holiness without which no one will see the Lord' (Hebrews 12 v 14). That is a posture worth imitating and a lead worth following."

SINCLAIR B. FERGUSON, Author, *Devoted to God;*
Chancellor's Professor of Systematic Theology, RTS

"This honest, humble and gentle book points us to follow in the footsteps of Christ and is a must-read, whether you've been in leadership for five minutes or fifty years. Rico offers a timely and timeless encouragement. With persuasive prose, engaging storytelling and practical and helpful advice and questions, he succinctly urges us to work hard at the things that matter: character, repentance, humility, gentleness and dependence on the Holy Spirit."

ELLIDH COOK, Student Worker, All Souls Langham Place, London

FAITHFUL LEADERS

AND THE THINGS THAT MATTER MOST

RICO TICE

thegoodbook
COMPANY

Faithful Leaders and the Things That Matter Most
© Rico Tice, 2021. Reprinted 2021, 2022.

Published by:
The Good Book Company

thegoodbook.com | thegoodbook.co.uk
thegoodbook.com.au | thegoodbook.co.nz | thegoodbook.co.in

Unless indicated, all Scripture references are taken from the Holy Bible, New International Version. Copyright © 2011 Biblica, Inc.™ Used by permission.

All rights reserved. Except as may be permitted by the Copyright Act, no part of this publication may be reproduced in any form or by any means without prior permission from the publisher.

Rico Tice has asserted his right under the Copyright, Designs and Patents Act 1988 to be identified as author of this work.

ISBN: 9781784985806 | Printed in the UK

Cover design by Jeff Miller, Faceout Studio | Art direction by André Parker

Contents

Foreword

+ + + + + + + + +

My best games of golf have all occurred when I am sound asleep. In dreamland I am capable of imaginary triumphs that bear no resemblance to my actual ability. The same is true, I fear, when it comes to assessing one's capacity for leadership. That is why the privilege of writing this foreword is tempered by being forced to face up to the challenge this book provides. I have been in pastoral ministry for 46 years, and the more the years pass, the more I understand that Christian leadership does not come naturally and never becomes easy.

When I think of leadership in general, I am put in mind of a fellow Scot. In October 2012, one of the Aldrich lecture halls at Harvard Business School was jam-packed; there was standing room only. No one was more surprised by the attendance than the visiting lecturer, Sir Alex Ferguson, who was speaking on the lessons in leadership he had learned in 26 years as manager of Manchester United.

One thing he emphasized has stuck with me since

I read his lecture: the care he took in choosing the captain of the team. Without a captain, a team loses direction and discipline just as an orchestra without a conductor forfeits coordination and harmony. In this, Sir Alex was not saying anything that the apostle Paul had not said 2,000 years before. Paul was equally clear that a leader of God's people must be possessed of a desire to lead, must command the respect of the team, must be clear about the "game plan" and must be capable of adapting to changing circumstances. Such a position of leadership—whether it be, as Rico says, around your dining table or from a pulpit—is no small thing, for it is to do God's work among God's people. But it is a great thing: "The saying is trustworthy: If anyone aspires to the office of overseer, he desires a noble task" (1 Timothy 3 v 1, ESV). Yet part of having a legitimate desire to lead is an almost inevitable emotional recoil—as sense of "Who is sufficient for these things?" Here is where, unlike leadership in some other spheres, Christian leadership demands humility. And it is in this happy tension between aspiration and an acknowledgment of personal inadequacy that faithful leadership is exercised.

So many of our problems in church life can be traced to defective leadership. Churches have too often been damaged by leaders who are exceptionally nice but afraid of their own shadow, and by those who are exceptionally driven but make others afraid of them. Those who have led God's people effectively are found in neither category. In writing to both Titus and Timothy, Paul urged them to make sure that they put the right leaders in place, and the way we lead matters no less today—because the church does not progress beyond the spiritual progress of its leaders.

It is essential that we get this right—and it is because Rico has his finger on the pulse that he is able to provide us with this wonderfully helpful guide to leadership. In print, as in person, he combines the forcefulness of a man who played rugby to a high level with a fetching sense of humility. He is aware that he has not written the "last word" on leadership, and he has certainly not written an easy word. But for those of us who long to lead effectively and faithfully, and who find that hard (and if we are honest, that is all of us), it is a necessary word.

One challenge contained in these pages is the way that Rico shows that effective leadership is not all about giftedness and ability. Fundamentally, he says, it is about holiness. In this, he is following the wisdom of men such as Robert Murray M'Cheyne and Charles Simeon. M'Cheyne, when he died at 29, left a legacy far greater than his age might suggest. In addressing the life of the minister/leader, he said, "My people's greatest need is my personal holiness". Simeon, a nineteenth-century minister in Cambridge, England, said that he heeded always the warning he was given by an older man:

> *"Watch continually over your own spirit, and do all in love; we must grow downwards in humility to soar heavenward. I should recommend your*

*having a watchful eye over yourself, for generally
speaking as is the minister so are the people."*

In other words, the key to the leader's public useful-
ness is his inner, unseen life. Character is what we are
when no one is looking. The leader is leading all the
time and, for the most part, unconsciously. Your holiness matters greatly to those you have been entrusted
to lead.

If the need for holiness is one challenge I shall take
from this book, the call to be faithful is another. I
am so glad that Rico chose the adjective "faithful" to
pair with the word "leadership". It is fairly common
for people to ask how they might pray for me in my
ministry, and as far back as I can remember my answer
has been the same: for faithfulness. Sometimes the response is to ask, "Faithfulness in what way?" to which I
tend to reply, "In every way!" Faithfulness to my wife,
my church family, to God's call, to God's word, to the
gospel... the *faithful* leader, as Rico so brilliantly de-
scribes in these pages, is the leader God is looking for,
and the leader who God will work through.

So you hold in your hands a book that will do you
great good—whether you are a pastor, a children's
teacher, a Bible-study leader, a seminary student... For
the church needs you to lead faithfully, and this book
will not only show you how to do so but inspire you
to do so. I often hear it observed that the future of the
church seems uncertain today because so many great
leaders are entering into their reward. But as J.C. Ryle
put it in his day:

"Fear not for the church when ministers die, and saints are taken away. Christ can ever maintain his own cause. He will raise up better servants and brighter stars. The stars are all in his right hand. Leave off all anxious thought about the future. All is going well, though our eyes may not see it. The kingdoms of this world shall yet become the kingdoms of our God and of his Christ."

I trust this short book will be part of the means by which God raises up leaders for this time who will be faithful to their call to love and serve God's church, for the furtherance of his kingdom and to the glory of his Son.

Alistair Begg
January 2021

Introduction

+ + + + + + + + +

One of the strange realities of being a pastor is that you spend more time at funerals than anyone else (apart from undertakers). Some are particularly joy-filled—celebrating a long life well-lived and now enjoyed into eternity. Some are particularly tear-stained—remembering a child, or a tragic self-inflicted death. Some are simply particularly memorable. So I'll never forget the funeral at which an old lady said to me, "Rico, do you know what failure is?" "No—tell me," I answered. What she said next has stuck with me ever since:

"Failure is being successful at the things that don't matter."

My best friend from university died in his thirties: he dropped dead of a pulmonary embolism. That was another memorable funeral, for all the wrong reasons. I remember standing at his graveside with his father, and his dad saying to me, "Rico, what do I write on my boy's grave? What epitaph do I put on there?"

The sobering truth is that one day, someone will have

15

to decide what epitaph to write on your gravestone too. I've been to a lot of funerals—one day people will gather at mine. Will they say I've been a success? What even is success? We all want it—no one wants to be known as and then remembered as a failure or a fool—but for Christian believers in a position of influence (whether that's around the family table at home or preaching from the pulpit in a church) what does success look like? What would failure be?

Here's what: the metric of success and failure is not what your relatives write on your gravestone but what God says to you that day you die. For to some he will say, "You fool," just as he did to the man in Jesus' parable who had lived as though his own self-advancement and self-gratification mattered most (Luke 12 v 20). And I don't think being a church member or a pastor insulates us from hearing that verdict. The fire of God's judgment will "test the quality of each person's work" in ministry (1 Corinthians 3 v 13). And…

"If it is burned up, the builder will suffer loss but yet will be saved—even though only as one escaping through the flames." (v 15)

There is a category of saved fool—of those who are saved by grace but whose lives were not well spent.

And yet to others our Lord will say, "Well done, good and faithful servant," just as was said to the men in Jesus' parable who used all that their master had given them to the uttermost, for his glory and their eternal joy (Matthew 25 v 21).

Of course, "it is by grace you have been saved, through faith—and this is not from yourselves, it is the gift of God—not by works, so that no one can boast" (Ephesians 2 v 8-9). I make sure I remind myself regularly of the three tenses of salvation that I learned when I was a young Christian. By grace I have been saved from the penalty of sin. By grace I am being saved from the power of sin. By grace I will one day be saved from the presence of sin.

But as trophies of grace, you and I are "created in Christ Jesus to do good works, which God prepared in advance for us to do" (Ephesians 2 v 10). My salvation is based only and always on Christ's finished work for me, but whether or not I hear "Well done" when I meet him is based on Christ's work through me—on my ministry in his service.

So just imagine hearing those words—that affirmation of your work from divine lips: "Well done". And just imagine hearing those words—that rebuke of your life from divine lips: "You fool". If God welcomes you into his presence on the cusp of eternity and fixes you in the eye and says, "You fool", all the achievements and accolades and accumulations of this life will not matter one jot. Failure is being successful at the things that don't matter. And if God welcomes you into his presence on the cusp of eternity and smiles at you and says, "Well done, good and faithful servant", then all the sacrifices and service and striving will have been infinitely, eternally worth it.

Hearing your Creator and your Father say, "Well

done"—that's all that ultimately matters, isn't it? That's the measure of a life worth living, whatever they say of me in a eulogy and whatever they write about me on my headstone.

This book is about what it takes to live that kind of life: what it looks like to hear "Well done" instead of "You fool". It is a book for anyone in any kind of church leadership. (I'll use the word "pastor" a lot—just substitute "elder", "youth worker", "Bible-study leader" or whatever applies to your own life.) It is by no means the last word on, or the only book you'll need about, Christian leadership. Nor is it (I hope) an easy read—I hope it will jolt you or change you. I'm not writing as someone who has all this sorted, but as a fellow struggler—from the trenches, as it were, rather than from the mountaintop. These are all things that I need to hear on repeat—and that you do too. Why? Because to a large extent, the spiritual health of a church leader determines the spiritual health of his congregation. That means that our success, our faithfulness, our progress and our leadership matter—and matter eternally.

I want to be a faithful leader. I want to hear my Father look me in the eye and, surveying my ministry, say, "Well done". I want you to hear it too. That means we need to define success, to fight our sin, to lead ourselves, and to serve our churches. Which sounds simple when I put it in a sentence; but, if you're like me, it's going to be the battle of our life.

+ + + + + + + + +

CHAPTER 1

DEFINE SUCCESS

+ + + + + + + + + +

Success is hearing "Well done" from the only lips that matter. Failure is being successful at things that don't truly matter at all.

You probably knew this already. But how hard it is to live it. How hard it is not to want the praise and affirmation now, here, from those around you and from your own heart. How hard it is not to count success in terms of the size of your house, the behaviour of your kids, or—perhaps most dangerous of all—the size or budget of your church or the publishing and sales of your books.

So, how does our Lord and Master define a successful ministry?

LEARNING FROM A PRISONER

By most measures, the apostle Paul had failed by the time he wrote his second letter to Timothy. He was in prison. He was facing execution. His followers were deserting him. The Christian communities he'd founded were struggling, riven with internal division and external persecution. Don't make the mistake of reading later history back into Paul's situation. He did not know, as he sat shivering in prison and writing to one of his few remaining friends, that the churches he had planted were the seeds of the fastest-multiplying religious explosion the world has ever seen. He did not know, as he contemplated his death at the hands of a Roman executioner, that one day that empire itself would not just tolerate but (for better and worse) promote Christianity. He did not know any of that, and by every worldly measure (including church-growth metrics) he had failed. His funeral would not be well-attended, there would be no obituaries printed lionising him, and the location of his grave would go unrecorded.

Yet Paul did not see his life as unsuccessful. And so he called Timothy to live a life of eternal success, even if it was likely to look like worldly failure. "Do your best to present yourself to God as one approved," he urged this younger pastor (2 Timothy 2 v 15). Live every day in a way that means that on that future day you'll hear the divine "Well done". How was Timothy to do that? How do we do that?

Two things: we must get the word right, and we must get our character right.

GET THE WORD RIGHT

The one of whom God approves is the one "who correctly handles the word of truth" (v 15). The word—Scripture—is the truth. That must be the lifelong anchor point of your ministry, for it is the only anchor point of a God-approved ministry. The Bible is the ultimate authority on doctrine and behaviour because it is the word of truth that God has breathed out (3 v 16). It originated in God's mind. It is what he has said. How dare we teach anything else? How arrogant for any preacher to have it read aloud in church, and then to stand up and base his sermon on anything other than what was read. This is what has happened in the last few generations in so many churches. The word is read, and then the preacher picks one or two phrases from the passage and uses them to justify their own thoughts.

No—success is a ministry of correctly handling the word of truth. And it can be correctly handled. How? First, Paul says, "Do your best". Be eager; be ready to put in the effort. You are a "worker". Anyone who wants to teach the word in any setting will need to be prepared to work at it—to put in the hard yards. In the previous chapter, Paul likens ministry to the life of a soldier, an athlete and a farmer. What links the three? All are called to disciplined, single-minded, patient work. If as a pastor I do not expect it will be hard work, then it should no longer be my work. Teaching the word is the same as farming: it takes time. The law of the field is that you plough, you sow, you water, you wait, you harvest. The law of teaching the word is that you give it time, you let it germinate in you before you share it with others, and so you never make the mistake of thinking you can prepare for Sunday on

Saturday night. As Dick Lucas, who was Rector of St Helen's Bishopsgate in London for many years, used to say to his young curates, "Shine the backside of your trousers off on your study chair".

The Greek word translated as "correctly handles" here is *orthotomounta*. It is, rather obviously, where we get our word "orthodoxy"; the original word, though, literally means "cuts straight". John Calvin said that we are to do with God's word what a father does with a loaf for his small children: he cuts it up for them so that they can digest and enjoy it. *Orthotomeo* was also used to describe how Roman roads, which famously cut straight through the countryside, were built. We are to cut the word straight, so that people can see it clearly and simply. We are not magicians pulling rabbits out of hats. It is our job to make the word plain, not mysterious. We do not want people to leave our sermons saying how clever or eloquent we are but how great Christ is. It takes more effort to do this than it does to make the word complex. To explain simply, you have to understand very deeply. Cut straight for the glory of God.

It may be that no one else will see the hard work that this requires from you. But God does. And you are, after all, working for him, and for approval in his sight. Paul tells us to "present yourself … as one approved" to God (2 v 15). That is, we labour not primarily for the present or future applause of our congregation, or our staff team, or the conference, or the reader. We work not for the approval of our mentor or our peers. I had the privilege of being on a church staff team with John Stott. And, to be honest, it was only when I visited him for the last time before he went to glory in 2011 that I realised that much of my ministry had been driven by the desire to hear his "Well done". And now that I never would hear that again, I remember asking myself, "Well, Rico, who are you doing this for?"

If you're a pastor, let me put it another way: if you knew that for the rest of your ministry you would have a church never larger than 50 members, receive no invitations to speak at church weekends away or conferences, sign no book deals, be asked onto zero podcasts and enjoy no applause from other ministers… would you work as hard at correctly handling the word of truth? That is the challenge. We must live for the approval of God, who sees the hard work that takes place as we sit on our study chair and are on our knees in prayer through the week just as much as he sees what we do when we are standing in the pulpit on a Sunday.

Then you will have nothing to be ashamed of on the day of judgment—that day when our ministry is judged and whether we built with gold and silver and precious stones or with wood and hay and straw is revealed (1 Corinthians 3 v 12-13). That day, the question will not be how much you grew the membership or the budget. It will not be how many people came to faith through your preaching. It will certainly not be how many column inches or social-media followers you gained. You know all that, I am guessing; and you find it hard to live remembering that, I am guessing. No, on the day of judgment, what will matter is if you taught the truth about grace, with grace—if your ministry reflected the one who came "full of grace and truth" (John 1 v 14). What will matter is whether you can say, "I worked hard to teach the Bible, despite what the culture said about it, despite what sometimes people in my congregation said about it, whatever ridicule I faced. I taught your word as you said it, Lord Jesus, and I taught your word with the grace with which you said it."

But not all pastors will be able to say that. And we're fools if we assume we will.

AN EASIER MINISTRY

A tragedy lies behind Paul's call to Timothy, for it comes against the backdrop of another type of ministry. There's always another—easier, more popular—approach to the word, which is to not cut a straight path through it but instead to swerve away from it. "Among them are Hymenaeus and Philetus, who have swerved from the truth … upsetting the faith of some" (2 Timothy 2 v 17-18, ESV). Paul is saying, *If Philetus is preaching, don't go to listen. If you're in Philetus' church, leave. If Hymenaeus is leading a Bible study or Sunday school class, I want you not to be there.* Their ministry "ruins the hearers" and it "will spread like gangrene" (v 14, 17). Theirs is a rapidly-growing ministry. And it's a ministry that is literally a catastrophe (v 14). This is a ministry that does not feed souls but rather feeds on souls.

False teaching is not just another point of view. It's gangrene. It'll lead to ruin—to spiritual shipwreck (1 Timothy 1 v 19). I was in Lahore, Pakistan, recently. It's a dangerous place to be a Christian: one of my events was cancelled because of a suicide-bomb threat, and that is just one of the risks that most Pakistani Christians face week by week. Towards the end of my trip, I asked a senior church leader what I could do to help him and the church there. There is such poverty in the church and the pressures on local Christians are so immense that it would have been a privilege to have been asked to fundraise. But he didn't ask me for money at all.

"We are being stopped from church planting by the Muslims here," he told me, "because they listen to what many of your bishops in the UK are saying about sexuality, and they think that we will teach the same as them, and not teach what will keep families together. So they won't let us plant churches.

"I don't want your money. I want your orthodoxy. I need you to be faithful."

False teaching has gangrenous effects far beyond what we can see or might imagine. And so we must oppose it in our own teaching, resisting the temptation to swerve from the truth; and we must stand against it in the teaching of others, resisting the temptation to think it does not really matter. When it comes to central gospel truth—who Jesus is, why he came, that he will come again—swerving is deadly. What must I do? I must be committed to "correcting [gospel] opponents with gentleness", praying that "God may perhaps grant them repentance leading to a knowledge of the truth" (2 Timothy 2 v 25). And I must be ready for others to speak that into my life too, and be ready to be brought back to the straight path if I ever swerve.

How does this catastrophic teaching creep in?

First, it happens when we start thinking like the world. The phrase in verse 16 translated "godless chatter" (NIV) or "irreverent babble" (ESV) is more closely translated as "profane talk"—"profane" being a word having its origins in "outside the temple". That is, profane means secular thinking—letting worldly priorities and views take precedence over biblical ones within the church.

I know that it is tempting to follow that road. All Souls Langham Place, the church where I serve in central London, is right next to the BBC, that beloved bastion of secular thinking in the UK. If we want to pull in a crowd here at All Souls, we will need to be a bit more tolerant, a bit more open, a bit more culturally attuned, a bit less confrontational, won't we? This church will never be successful if we don't take account of where the culture is at and just flex our message to it, right?

That's how you start to swerve. You'll know your own context, and you need to work out how this temptation looks for you.

Then second, when we start thinking like the world, we soon enough begin speaking like the world. In the case of Hymenaeus and Philetus, that meant preaching that the resurrection had already taken place. The dominant Greek culture of the time could not handle a bodily resurrection, and through the ages no cultural elite has ever particularly welcomed the idea of a judgment day in which they might be on the wrong side of the divide. So the false teaching that everyone can experience resurrection life right now, with all its benefits—an end to pain, toil and difficulty, and a life of continual wholeness and victory—was going to go down well in the first-century Roman world. And it was going to be particularly popular when held up next to the message from Paul—a prisoner facing execution—that "we must go through many hardships to enter the kingdom of God" (Acts 14 v 22). Which message looks more likely to lead to growth? Which is more like to be successful?

False teaching dazzles, then it distorts, then it diverts, and finally it destroys. Those are the four stages, time and again. So first of all, it dazzles, and people rush toward it. The old message in their old church seems dull compared to the show up the road. There's a sense of excitement. It looks as if God is moving. But false teaching distorts. Perhaps only by degrees, but walk for a while along a path that has swerved by a few degrees and you end up a long way from the narrow path. The gap gradually widens. *We've been raised and we can now enjoy all the fruits of resurrection—here and now. Live a life of victory! God wants so much more for you!* And so false teaching diverts. *I can live free of suffering. I'm not sure why I'd want to listen to Paul—he's in prison, and his teaching is, well, a bit negative. No, I'm going to live a life of victory over turmoil, temptations, sadness, sickness.*

And then it destroys.

I've lost my job. I prayed for my mother, and she still died. We wanted kids, and they never came. I am still struggling with that temptation. God never did what he said he would. The life he promised never showed up, not for me. He doesn't love me. I'm not good enough. Is he even there? This isn't worth it. I'm out.

False teaching can look like explicitly denying scriptural truths; but more subtly, and therefore more dangerously, it can mean simply not ever mentioning some culturally or personally unpalatable scriptural truths—that is, not warning as well as teaching (Colossians 1 v 28, ESV)—not teaching the whole counsel of God (Acts 20 v 27, ESV). I recently spoke with someone who had done an in-depth study into the teaching at a very large megachurch, and his conclusion was that they did not preach what they believed—some truths seemed likely to inhibit growth, so they were downplayed or never taught about at all. (There's no "happy ending" here—the church's leaders decided not to make any changes, though one senior leader there courageously resigned in response to that decision.) This kind of failure to mention hard truths is harder to spot than an outright denial of those truths (in our own teaching as well as in someone else's). But both methods of teaching are false, and both destroy. We must preach what we believe, and preach all that we believe.

So swerving comes from thinking like the world and then speaking like the world. But third and most terrifyingly, swerving happens when I assume it cannot happen to me. Notice that Paul assumes Timothy knows who he is talking about when he names Hymenaeus and Philetus. These men were not strangers: they had been ministry partners. Neither was Demas, who was with Paul and Luke as Paul wrote to the Colossian church and to his friend Philemon (Colossians 4 v 14; Philemon v 24), and yet, by the time of this letter, he was tragically "in love with this present world [and had] deserted me and gone" (2 Timothy 4 v 10). So here's the issue. These men knew the truth. There had been a day when they taught a faithful Bible study, when they preached a faithful sermon, when they cut the word straight... but gradually, inch by inch, they had wandered away from it.

I haven't done any scientific work on the data here, but my sense from several decades in ministry is that most of the high-profile and dangerous false teachers today were not false teachers when they started out. In other words, they were once committed to the truths that you and I are. They once cut the word straight. Are you more gifted or more educated or more hard-working than them? Probably not. If it can happen to Hymenaeus, it can happen to Timothy. If it can happen to [insert name of a current teacher who tragically swerved here], it can happen to you.

So what is the response to this reality? "Do your best to present yourself to God as one approved, a workman who does not need to be ashamed, who correctly handles the word of truth." Leave no stone unturned in your efforts to get the word right, Paul tells his younger friend. One huge blessing for me in this regard has been our church's Thursday morning preaching group. Anyone in the staff team can come, and Sunday's preacher preaches his sermon to them, and then invites their feedback for 20 minutes. I can think of times when that feedback has sent me back to the passage to work harder at it; and other times when it has changed how I say what needs to be said from the text. Preaching prep is not a private activity, to be kept under wraps and only unveiled only when you step into the pulpit. I'm always amazed by pastors who pray, prepare and preach, and only then receive feedback. It's too late by then. For 25 years, that Thursday morning meeting has kept me cutting the word straight.

Remember what success is. Get the word right. Keep teaching it. Keep working hard at it. Keep bringing yourself back to it and allowing others to bring you back to it. Keep working for God's "Well done" and no one else's.

And make sure your character matches up with your teaching.

CHARACTER MATTERS

The Scriptures nowhere call men to teach truth without also commanding them to live it out. In 1 Timothy 3 v 2-7, when Paul lists out the qualifications for being an "overseer", there are twelve that speak to character or relationships, and only one about teaching. For those of us who are "able to teach", it is easy to read a line like "We must get the word right, and we must get our character right" and focus far more on the first clause than the second. But one out of two is not a pass mark here. A leader's character must never be an afterthought, nor can strengths in teaching justify or make up for weaknesses in conduct. A friend of mine who pastors a large church recently commented that a lot of the weaknesses in evangelical leadership stem from an emphasis on teaching and gifting but not on character and godliness. God's word never gives us leave to do that.

2 Timothy 2 is no different. Having told Timothy to cut the word straight, Paul moves straight on to character. He conjures up the image of a great house, and as in any great house (think Downton Abbey) there are a huge number of "articles"—"some are for special purposes and some for common use" (2 Timothy 2 v 20). Some are going to be useful for glorious tasks: others, useless for anything that is worth anything. And Paul is saying to Timothy, and to every single Christian, *Be useful.* How? "Those who cleanse themselves from the latter [worthless purposes] will be instruments for special purposes, made holy, useful to the Master" (v 21). The great house is the people of God, and essentially the question is: will I be a silver platter or will I be a binbag? Will I be useful to the Master or not? And the key to "cleanliness" here is not the quality of my teaching but the godliness of my character—my holiness. It is character that holds a lasting ministry together.

What marks out the person of godly character? First, they have quick feet: "Flee the evil desires of youth and pursue righteousness, faith, love, and peace along with those who call on the Lord out of a pure heart" (v 22). The godly person is able to run in two directions. He or she flees the evil desires of youth (a word Paul is probably using to mean those aged under 40). The idea here is of immature desires: impatience with the status quo, self-assertion, aversion to rule and routine, grudging obedience to authority or unmanageable tendencies. These tend to be the marks of younger people (though we will all know those who did not grow out of them as they grew older, and those who by God's grace were not marked by them even when they were young in years.) And it's appropriate to note here that sometimes—often, tragically—it's in the area of sex that the immature desires of youth play themselves out most destructively.

Paul says, *Learn to spot these desires in yourself, and flee them instead of feeding them.*

As well as fleeing *from* evil desires, we're to use our spiritual legs to "pursue righteousness, faith, love and peace". And how do you pursue them? "Along with those who call on the Lord out of a pure heart." In other words, godly character does not grow in a rugged individualist.

That is, the pastor cannot take as his model James Bond or most characters in Westerns played by Clint Eastwood—yet so often, we do. Bond and Clint never have friends, do they? (Well, they do, occasionally—

but their friends almost invariably get shot before the end of the film.) They're alone. They fight and they win on their own. They're not accountable to anyone for anything. And the problem is when we operate like that in real life, we lose on our own. So often I meet up with men who've just wrecked their ministry or their career or their marriage in some way, and as I talk to them, I realise, "You haven't let anyone in. You have fought on your own, and you've lost on your own." Godly character grows in the pack, not in lone wolves. And if you are reading this and you are thinking, "I'm ok, and openness and accountability and pursuing friendships are not really my thing", then let me tell you something: Satan's thrilled.

KINDNESS IS NON-NEGOTIABLE

Alongside quick feet, we need clean lips. "The Lord's servant must not be quarrelsome but must be kind to everyone, able to teach, not resentful" (v 24). Eugene Peterson helpfully renders this verse like this:

"God's servant must not be argumentative, but a gentle listener and a teacher who keeps cool, working firmly but patiently with those who refuse to obey." (The Message)

"A teacher who keeps cool." A lifetime of ministry can be lost through the misuse of a few words. A God-approved pastorate can be compromised by a constant desire to quarrel. Yes, we must contend for the gospel and we must stand and oppose people who teach against the gospel. Kindness and firmness are not opposites. But this does not mean that every disagreement over secondary issues must lead to a public quarrel. It does not mean that every hill is one to die upon. It does not mean that every Twitter controversy requires our contribution. And it certainly does not mean that kindness can ever be sacrificed in the cause of defending truth. It *does* mean that we will contend in a way that is gracious—rather than preaching sermonettes at individuals.

Often the best way to do that is to ask people questions, helping them to see what the trajectory of their opinion is or how it contradicts a basic tenet of the gospel. Fundamentally, here is the question: do you speak kindly to and about those who make your ministry most difficult? Will you be someone with clean lips or one with an uncontrollable tongue?

After all, we follow a Lord who came not to be served but to serve. A few years ago, there was a TV series called "An Edwardian Country House"—six episodes of reality TV in which people lived in a house from 100 years ago, either as master and mistress or as the servants. There was a very strict code of conduct, based on the old British class system. One rule for the master and mistress was this:

> *"If by chance you meet a lower servant, you should walk past leaving them unnoticed. You'll spare them the shame of explaining their presence."*

And here was one of the rules for the lower servants:

*"If you meet one of your betters in the house,
endeavour to make yourself invisible, give room,
turn your back and avert your eyes."*

We recoil from that. But let's not pretend that we
wouldn't rather be the master in that setting than the
servant—or that a pastor doesn't enjoy a position that
allows him to indulge that preference to be the master
from time to time (or, if unchecked, a lot of time). Pastors, as recent and very sad stories have shown, are not
immune from expecting to go unchallenged in their
decisions, from treating others as less important or
dispensable, from silencing those who don't agree with
them or from failing to notice those who are "lower".
I need to ask myself: if I asked my church members,
would they say, "Yes, this guy is kind to everyone—and
when he is not, he is quick to own it, apologise, and
make amends"?

WELL DONE

So the key to a ministry that is useful to the Master
is not less than teaching the word faithfully, but it is
more than that. The key is not academic qualifications
or rhetorical eloquence or inspirational vision-casting.
It is godliness. Many of us subconsciously find that un-
appealing, I think, because it's harder work, and longer
work, to clean our characters. It's less noticed and more
rarely praised. (When did you hear a Christian conference speaker welcomed to the platform by reference
first and foremost not to their titles, their preaching
abilities, or their writing successes but to their godly

character?) That's the call—to cut the word straight, and to get our character clean.

Most of us will know people who exemplify this approach to ministry, and it's wonderful to see. I think instantly of the man who led me to Christ—kind, patient, unresentful, gently teaching me and many others.

As the blogger, author and elder Tim Challies puts it:

> *"The highest privilege and greatest honour in pastoring is not standing in the church pulpit but praying by the hospital bed. It's not being accorded the highest place but carrying out the least-seen service. It's not broadcasting the truth to thousands, but whispering it to one. The holiest moments of pastoring are the ones that are seen by the fewest people. And in the end, I'm convinced these are the ones that mean the most. Most people will forget most of your sermons, but they'll remember that when they called, you came. They'll remember that you were there when their hearts were broken, that you were there to lead them to the Lord and to speak his truth into their sorrows."*
>
> *(challies.com/articles/the-celebrity-pastor-weve-never-known/, accessed June 23rd, 2020)*

That is a successful life, for that is a successful ministry. The world, and indeed the wider church or even your own church, may not notice it or thank you for it. The world—and, tragically, many professing Christians—will tend to applaud those whose characters are more worldly than godly, or whose teaching is more inspired by what the world says than what the Scriptures say. But that will mean nothing in 200 years. "Do your best to present yourself to God as one approved, a worker who does not need to be ashamed and who correctly handles the word of truth." Failure is being successful at the wrong things; and success for the pastor is standing before his Shepherd one day, after a life of cutting the word straight and living with clean character, and hearing those precious words that will sustain his joy for eternity:

"Well done, good and faithful servant."

+ + + + + + + + +

CHAPTER 2

FIGHT YOUR SIN

+ + + + + + + + +

Have you ever felt genuine, real fear? I unashamedly hope this chapter will cause that: that it will produce not butterflies in your stomach but rather an eagle in your gut. No other passage in the whole of the Old Testament has scarred me and shaped me like the one from which Billy Graham chose to speak to his leadership, staff and counsellors before his mission at Harringay, London, back in 1954.

It's the story of Achan from Joshua 7. Dr Graham had the whole Bible to speak from as he prepared those who would help him with the two-month mission that would, by God's grace, see two million people attend and 40,000 profess faith. And he chose this part of the history of God's people entering the promised land 3,000 years ago. Isn't that extraordinary? Why did he pick this?

Because holiness mattered for his mission, and it matters for your ministry.

STOP PRAYING

Let me take you back to the borders of Canaan as Joshua leads the people of Israel into the promised land after 40 years in the wilderness. We are picking up the story just after the miraculous fall of the stronghold of Jericho. If ever there were a moment that assured the Israelites that they really would be given the land, surely it was when they watched the walls fall down as God moved to give them the city. "The LORD was with Joshua, and his fame spread throughout the land" is how the final verse of Joshua 6 ends (v 27).

Next it's the turn of Ai—a strategic town in the centre of the land. To continue the conquest, Ai needs to be taken. But it's a small town and ought to fall with very little resistance; Joshua's scouts report back to him that "not all the army will have to go up against Ai. Send two or three thousand men to take it ... for only a few people live there" (7 v 3).

You can imagine Joshua heaving a sigh of relief. He can delegate this operation to a junior lieutenant. He can give most of his soldiers a day off. Jericho, that mighty citadel, fell without a single casualty—Ai will be easy.

> *"So about three thousand went up; but they were routed by the men of Ai, who killed about thirty-six of them. They chased the Israelites from the city gate as far as the stone quarries and struck them down on the slopes." (v 4-5)*

This is the only defeat recorded in the book of Joshua; it is the only time in this book that God's people are slain in battle. And "at this the hearts of the people melted in fear and became like water" (v 5). Up to this point, only their enemies' hearts had melted in fear, as Rahab, the inhabitant of Jericho who had switched sides, had told Joshua's spies:

> *"I know that the LORD has given you the land, and that the fear of you has fallen upon us, and that all the inhabitants of the land melt away before you. For we have heard how the LORD dried up the water of the Red Sea before you when you came out of Egypt, and what you did to the two kings of the Amorites who were beyond the Jordan, to Sihon and Og, whom you devoted to destruction. And as soon as we heard it, our hearts melted, and there was no spirit left in any man because of you, for the LORD your God, he is God in the heavens above and on the earth beneath." (2 v 9-11, ESV)*

Later:

> *"When all the Amorite kings west of the Jordan and all the Canaanite kings along the coast heard how the LORD had dried up the [River] Jordan before the Israelites until they had crossed over, their hearts melted in fear and they no longer had the courage to face the Israelites." (5 v 1)*

Of course they didn't: they knew what they were up against—the LORD God. But now in chapter 7 the boot is on the other foot. And so "Joshua tore his clothes

and fell face down to the ground before the ark of the
LORD, remaining there till evening. The elders of Israel
did the same, and sprinkled dust on their heads" (7
v 6). It's a serious, sombre prayer meeting. And they are
perplexed, because somehow they have snatched defeat
from the jaws of victory. *Why did you bring us here,
God, if we're going to be defeated,* Joshua asks. *What can
I say when everyone around us will hear what happened
at Ai? They'll surround us and wipe us out.* "What then
will you do for your own great name?" (v 9).

And then something shocking happens.

> "The LORD said to Joshua, 'Stand up! What are
> you doing down on your face?'" (v 10)

I know of no other place in the Bible where God says to
someone, *Stop praying.* That's what he says here, though.
*Joshua, cancel this prayer meeting. Instead, get your Bible
out, and you will see what is going on here.* Why? "Israel
has sinned; they have violated my covenant, which I
commanded them to keep." How? "They have taken
some of the devoted things; they have stolen, they have
lied, they have put them with their own possessions.
That is why the Israelites cannot stand against their enemies; they turn their backs and run because they have
been made liable to destruction" (v 11-12).

And then the real kick:

> "I will not be with you any more." (v 12)

Can you imagine God saying that to you? "I will not
be with you any more."

42

Joshua needs to stop praying, and he needs to judge the situation by the word of God and deal with the problem. There was a clear divine instruction in 6 v 18: "Keep away from the devoted things, so that you will not bring about your own destruction by taking any of them. Otherwise you will make the camp of Israel liable to destruction and bring trouble on it." And there has been a straightforward disobedience of that command: "Achan son of Karmi, the son of Zimri, the son of Zerah, of the tribe of Judah, took some of [the devoted things]" and buried them underground in his tent (7 v 1, 21).

The problem is sin, and the sin needs to be dealt with, and all the prayers in the world will make no difference until it is.

The American Baptist preacher Dr Al Martin used to tell the story of a local pastor's church. One member, an old man, would come each week to the church's prayer meeting, and each week he would zealously pray, "Oh Lord, the old spider of sin, the old spider of sin has been weaving its web; it's been weaving its web. Lord, break the web, break the web." Every time, every week, the same prayer—until one evening, as this old man was praying, "Break the web," the pastor cracked and shouted out, "No Lord, kill the spider!"

Kill the spider. Kill the sin. All the prayers in the world will make no difference to those who will not kill their sin.

This is personal for me. I am a British Anglican, and our leadership keep calling for prayer, but when it comes to sexual ethics, they will not judge the situation in our denomination by the word of God: they will not state that the only place for sex is between a man and a woman within marriage, and that the only other God-honouring option is celibacy. And this issue is crucial because it is one where Western culture and the Bible are more and more in opposition. This is one of the areas where we are under most pressure to bow the knee to "Caesar" in our day, and so this will be the place where we are most likely to capitulate, to go with the flow, to keep our heads down and compromise on truth.

In the Anglican church in England, there's endless prayer, and yet time and again there is total disobedience of Scripture in this area. We have our prayer meetings, but we will not call people to repent of their sin. It was for this reason that I felt I had to resign from the Archbishop of Canterbury's Commission on Evangelism. The Vice-chair, whom the archbishop had appointed, refused to call same-sex couples to repent. Evangelism is a subsection of faithfulness, and so evangelism that is not accompanied by obedience is not faithful to the Lord we're proclaiming. And so I resigned, saying, "You are not telling people they need to repent, but you keep calling for prayer meetings. How do you expect the Holy Spirit to be with us in this?"

IT WILL FIND YOU OUT

Let's walk through this with Achan for a while. He was there on the front line in Jericho. He saw the walls tumble, and he entered the city. A friend of mine who's a soldier and has seen active service once told me that in the chaos and commotion of battle there are some moments of extreme isolation when everything seems to stand still. So picture Achan charging up a street with his fellow Israelite warriors, and turning aside on his own to go into a house to clear it. And he lingers for a moment in this quiet solitude of the front room. There's no one there. And he tells Joshua later on what happens: "When I saw in the plunder a beautiful robe from Babylonia, two hundred shekels of silver and a bar of gold weighing fifty shekels, I coveted them and took them" (v 21). He's seen what, in our terms, would be tens of thousands of pounds' worth of plunder. And as he stood there in that front room, isolated for a moment amid all the commotion, we can imagine him saying to himself, *Well, no one will notice. No one can see. What a waste. We're going to burn this robe? God can't really mean that. Battles are for taking plunder.* And he looked, he longed, and he took.

Why? Because at that moment, he was not worshipping the God of Israel but was instead worshipping an idol. Before him was the means to financial security. He'd spent years going without, in the wilderness. Now, suddenly, here was the chance not only to live in the promised land but to live well in the promised land. Here was, in our terms, the paying off of the mortgage, the exotic trips, the college fees and pension pot, and all the status and respect that goes with having made it. His heart had been captured by his dreams and his nightmares—dreams of prosperity, nightmares of penury. He presumably didn't realise it. He'd presumably never asked himself, "What do I feel I can't live without? What might I risk everything to get or keep? What am I at risk of worshipping as my god?" Therefore, at the point of temptation he was profoundly vulnerable. And he sinned. You can imagine him creeping back into Jericho under cover of darkness that night, going back to that house, grabbing all the treasure and then tip-toeing back into the Israelite camp, heart pounding, reaching his tent, showing his wife, waking the kids to bury the treasure under their beds, and then experiencing a flood of joy and relief. You can see him putting his arm round his wife and saying, *We've done it. We've made it.*

And then imagine that two days later, Achan is given the day off from the battle for Ai. His friend in the next-door tent is not. They're family friends. And Achan's friend bids farewell, telling his wife he'll be home for lunch—it's only Ai!—and he doesn't give his kids a kiss goodbye because the LORD is for his people. And later that day, they bring his body back.

And then Achan must have heard, along with the rest of the camp, the dread words: "There are devoted things among you, Israel. You cannot stand against your enemies until you remove them" (v 13). Joshua tells the people how the perpetrator will be identified: the next day, God will identify his tribe, then his clan, then his family, and then the man. God will put his hand on the culprit—but he gives him time. Achan has a whole night before he is identified.

What will Achan do? Will he remember Numbers 32 v 23: "You may be sure that your sin will find you out"? Will he remember the truth that came to be written so poetically in Psalm 139? "You discern my going out and my lying down; you are familiar with all my ways" (v 3). Through the night, Achan is in what John Bunyan would, over two millennia later, call the Valley of Decision. He has seen God's power and kindness in the wilderness. He has seen the manna and the quail provided for the people by their God each day. He has seen the Jordan River being dried up by the power of God so they can cross into the land. Only 72 hours before, he walked round Jericho seven times, he shouted, and he saw God bring the walls down.

What will he do? Will he confess and humbly beg for mercy? Or will he try to get away with it?

He closes his heart to all that he knows of God. He decides to pin his hopes on God not knowing. Perhaps he says to his wife, *No one saw. No one knows. We can get away with this. It may still be ok.* So when morning comes, he just lines up with his family, in his clan, as part of his tribe.

Graham Daniels, a friend of mine who is an evangelist, told me of a time when he went to do a talk about Jesus at a school in the south of England, and he was waiting outside the headmaster's office to meet him before the assembly. Next to him was sitting a nervous-looking boy. Graham said, "Any problems?" And the boy answered:

> *"Yes, yesterday when the bell went for the end of the school day, somebody took a fire extinguisher off the wall and squirted it everywhere."*

And Graham, noting this boy's nervousness and the fact that he was standing outside the headteacher's office, said to him, "Ah, and did you do it?"

And the boy replied, "I don't know."

I don't know?! He'd done it—but he was sitting there outside the headmaster's office, deciding whether he was going to try to bluff the headmaster. (Graham found out later that he'd sprayed a third of the school and the Vice-head had seen him do it. Sadly, he never found out whether the boy decided to play the "I don't know" defence with his headmaster, nor how any attempt at bluffing went.) Here, Achan is going to try to bluff... God.

Can you imagine the adrenaline rush the next morning as Achan lines up with the rest of the tribe of Judah and the result of the first lot is called...

> *Judah!*

All the other tribes draw back, and now Achan starts to feel nervous, and he can feel the sweat dripping down his back.

And the lot is drawn again...

> *Zerahites!*

And he hears his wife stifle a little cry and clasp their baby to her chest.

And the lot is drawn again…

Zimri!

And now Achan can hardly stand.

And the lot is drawn again…

Achan!

Be sure that your sin will find you out.

Achan finally confesses—he has no choice. They find the devoted things hidden in his tent, and they bring it all, along with Achan and his family, to the Valley of Achor. And Joshua, perhaps pointing to 36 freshly dug graves as he does so, says to Achan, "'Why have you brought this trouble on us? The LORD will bring trouble on you today.' Then all Israel stoned him, and after they had stoned the rest, they burned them" (Joshua 7 v 25). And as I read that, I think of my own family— my wife, my two sons and my daughter. And I think of them saying, "Daddy, what has your sin done? What has your sin done to us? Daddy, what did you do?"

Be sure that your sin will find you out.

YOUR SIN MATTERS

I hope there is an eagle in your guts. There is in mine— because God takes sin among his people no less seriously today than he did then. And so your sin matters. It matters first because sin is adulterous. "The Israelites were unfaithful" (7 v 1). Sin is spiritual cheating on the

God who created us, saved us, dwells with us and will one day glorify us in his presence. That is the measure of his love for us. And when we think and act like the world out of which he has saved us—be it in our sexual lives (or thoughts), or our coveting and taking what is not ours, or in our using our ministries to point to our own greatness rather than his glory, or anything else—that is adultery. It is why James calls Christians "You adulterous people" and explains that "friendship with the world means enmity against God? Therefore, anyone who chooses to be a friend of the world becomes an enemy of God" (James 4 v 4).

Sam Allberry says it well:

> "We are to think of the horror of a husband
> or wife discovering their spouse in the midst
> of an affair. James says that such horrendous
> behaviour aptly describes what Christians do
> when they turn their back on God … Christians
> two-time God when we adopt the values of the
> world. God takes [this] personally—just like a
> husband who finds his wife back in bed with
> the thug she was dating before he had come
> into her life and rescued her from that awful
> relationship. Such a husband would have every
> right to be angry. And James is very clear that
> being unfaithful to God provokes his enmity."
> (James For You, page 109)

A pastor once told me about a woman who had told him she was having an affair. She said to him that whenever she committed adultery in her home, she would put her husband's picture face down so she didn't have eye contact with her husband when her lover was there. Of course, it was just a picture—but she wanted to exclude her husband's gaze from that area of her life. She didn't want him looking at her, as it were, as she took her lover to their bed.

When I sin, I am acting as though, in this area of my life, I can put God face down so that he will not see. That is essentially what Achan had convinced himself of. He had compartmentalised his life and allowed sin to rule just one part, as though he could keep that part from God. I'm sure he still intended to go to religious services. I'm sure he still wanted to be part of the people of God. It was just that he had decided that his wealth was his own, to gather as he saw fit and use as he saw fit. Find a fallen pastor and you will usually find a pastor who simply did not let God speak into one area of his life—and that is one area too many. What we are like backstage must be no different to who we are when we're on stage.

When I sin, I am functionally believing that God cannot see—or I am functionally ignoring the reality that I am committing spiritual adultery. But he sees all of me, and he calls my sin for what it is. Be sure that your adultery will find you out. If I were to remember each time I am tempted to live for my glory rather than for God's that what I am being tempted to do is to commit spiritual adultery, I imagine I would resist temptation much more successfully.

IT MATTERS FOR *THEM*

Second, sin matters because sin is corporate. "*The Israelites* were unfaithful in regard to the devoted things; Achan son of Karmi..." (Joshua 7 v 1, my emphasis). Achan had sinned, but actually God's verdict was not just that Achan had sinned; it was that Israel had sinned. Achan stole the gold, the silver and the beautiful robe, but "the Israelites were unfaithful". All the way through the first half of the chapter, God addresses Israel as a nation: "*They* have taken some of the devoted things; *they* have stolen, *they* have lied, *they* have put them with their own possessions. That is why *the Israelites* cannot stand" (v 11-12, my emphasis). Sin is corporate; and to a certain measure, so is judgment. It is not only Achan, or Achan and his wife, upon whom God's anger falls. It is his whole family; and, had Achan's sin not been dealt with, it would have been the whole of Israel. This is very hard for us to grasp because we live in such a profoundly individualistic culture, in which so many family units are disjointed or distanced. But we have to reckon with the truth that the sin of Achan had a profound impact on the whole congregation of Israel. His family, and 36 men, died as a result of it. As Joshua would one day recall, "When Achan son of Zerah was unfaithful in regard to the devoted things, did not wrath come on the whole community of Israel? He was not the only one who died for his sin" (Joshua 22 v 20).

God will not dwell in the midst of sin, and we cannot expect him to bless his people when sin goes unchallenged and undealt with. So he withdrew himself from the presence of his people.

The 17th-century poet John Donne famously wrote, "No man is an island entire of itself; every man is a piece of the continent, a part of the main". That principle runs right through the Bible. This is the issue. Sin is contagious; it is radioactive. Like false teaching, it spreads like gangrene. My sin affects you, and your sin affects me. As Paul put it to a church that tolerated sexual immorality in its midst, and even celebrated that tolerance, "Don't you know that a little yeast leavens the whole batch of dough? Get rid of the old yeast" (1 Corinthians 5 v 6-7).

Unlike Old Testament Israel in Joshua's time, as God's people we're not commanded to destroy things Jesus hates, or stone those who disobey Jesus. Jesus will bring God's judgment as and when he sees fit. Nor are we to assume that disappointment in ministry or mission is always and only the result of unrepented sin. But the Bible is nevertheless clear that God will not be with those who tolerate, excuse or belittle sin's presence among his people.

So, in the book of Revelation, Jesus warns churches not to tolerate things that he hates; or he, the light of the world, will come and remove his "lampstand"—that is, withdraw his presence from among them so that his light shines neither to nor through them. In his letter to the Ephesians the Lord warns them, "Consider how far you have fallen! Repent and do the things you did at first. If you do not repent, I will come to you and remove your lampstand from its place" (Revelation 2 v 5). And he gives this warning even though they are working hard, persevering, enduring hardships for their faith and standing against some sins (v 2-3, 6). To the believers in Pergamum, the Lord of heaven says, "There are some among you who hold to the teaching [that promotes] sexual immorality … Repent therefore! Otherwise, I will soon come to you and will fight against them" (v 14, 16). To Thyatira, he says, "I have this against you: you tolerate that woman Jezebel … By her teaching she misleads my servants into sexual immorality and the eating of food sacrificed to idols. I have given her time to repent of her immorality, but she is unwilling. So I will cast her on a bed of suffering, and I will make those who commit adultery with her suffer intensely, unless they repent of her ways … Then all the churches will know that I am he who searches hearts and minds" (v 20-23). The problem with the majority in this church is not that they commit these sins, or approve of these sins, but that they tolerate them. That's how serious sin is—so serious that it is also sinful to wink at it or overlook it.

The warning is this: the Holy Spirit will depart unless we name our sin for what it is and then deal with it accordingly. Bishop Handley Moule once warned that, "At the heart of all heresy is an inadequate view of sin". Your sin matters not just for you but for your whole church. Your sin may be a private thing to you but it is not private to God, and it affects your family and your whole church. And if it is not dealt with, then do not be surprised to find Jesus acting to discipline you (plural), and do not be surprised if even the tiniest spiritual objective becomes impossible for you (plural).

A while back I was part of an evangelism initiative at a church and it was not bearing fruit. I remember thinking, "Lord, there are so few people professing faith. It seems so hard." And then one of the people on staff at that church collapsed and was taken to hospital. It was discovered that he had an STD, and then it came out that he'd been visiting brothels and massage parlours, and that only came to light because the medics wouldn't release him from hospital unless his flatmate was told, and his flatmate came and told his pastors. And when this man—a guy who was on staff at this church—was asked what was going on, he essentially said, "It's nothing to do with you. That's my private time and my private life." But the truth is it had everything to do with that church, because sin is corporate. And that is surely why Billy Graham made sure his team was aware of the danger of hidden, unconfessed, unrepentant sin before the mission began—because sin is adulterous, and sin is corporate.

So, what are you hiding under your tent? Sexual immorality of some kind? Sins driven by covetousness, as in Achan's case? Your sin affects your family and your church. The health of the church depends on the health of the pulpit. Be sure that your sin will find you out. What are you hiding? And what will you do with it?

I hope the eagle is flying in your gut right now.

DON'T BLUFF GOD

The question for us is not whether we sin. We do. Pastors we may be, but perfect we are not. The question is what we will do about it.

First, don't bluff God. Confess. Act as though 1 John 1 v 8-9 is actually true, and true for you no less than for your church members (I've put it into a direct form, to let it hit home):

> *"If you claim to be without sin, you deceive yourself and the truth is not in you. If you confess your sin, he is faithful and just and will forgive you your sins and purify you from all unrighteousness."*

Church members are unlikely to be repentant unless their leaders are repentant. The pastor and theologian Jack Miller famously put it like this: "If the pastor is not the chief repenter, the gospel becomes a theoretical solution for the theoretical problem of sin, for theoretical sinners—should there be any present".

Don't bluff God. Repent before him. And, if you have sinned against someone else, repent to them; and if you have sinned publicly, then repent publicly. This means saying sorry, without caveat or excuse. If your church or organisation has sinned corporately then, again, say sorry publicly and fully. Wade Mullen, who teaches at Lancaster Bible College in Pennsylvania and has done a great deal of research into how institutions respond when wrongdoing is revealed, is helpful here: he identifies several forms of apologies that are in fact non-apologies. There is the one that condemns (suggesting there is no need to apologise: "I'm sorry you feel that way"), the one that appeases (that is, it's offered only because it's in your best interests), the one that excuses, the one that justifies, the one that self-promotes (pitching for ongoing support from people, and even from victims) and the one that asks for sympathy ("This has been very hard for everyone"; "We are hurting too"). Perhaps we need to learn how to say sorry properly, both in our hearts and with our lips. Mullen is again very helpful on what real repentance looks like, before God and before people. It requires you to surrender (that is, give up defending yourself), confess (name the wrongs), own it (take responsibility and acknowledge there will be consequences), recognise it (name the harms that the wrongs have caused), empathise (feel the weight of what you've done) and then "out of that broken place of surrender, confession, ownership, recognition, and empathy might emerge the words, 'We are so sorry'" (wadetmullen.com/what-ive-observed-when-institutions-try-to-apologize-and-how-they-can-do-better/, accessed 1st February 2021).

You cannot bluff God. Most of the time, you cannot bluff people, either. They usually know when repentance is real and when it is not. God *always* knows.

HE WAS CRUSHED FOR *YOUR* INIQUITIES

Achan died for his sin, but you need not. When we are confronted by our sin and stop making excuses for it or hiding from it, there are two things we can do. One is that we get knocked over by it and we stay down on the mat. The other is that we get knocked over but we allow God to lift us up, to forgive us and to enable us to fight again. Achan was taken out of the camp, and he was stoned, but amazingly the Lord Jesus has died for your sin.

Jesus was taken out of the camp and killed for you. All Achan's sin was laid out—all the treasure that he had stolen from God. And the Bible says the same will be true for us: "There is nothing concealed that will not be disclosed, or hidden that will not be made known" (Luke 12 v 2). Some of us are very good at hiding our sin from others and even from ourselves, but he sees it all, and to him we must give an account. Our sin is laid out before God—and then the Son of God was crushed for it. He was pierced for your transgressions. He was crushed for your iniquities. The punishment that brought you peace was upon him. By his wounds you are healed. So confess your sin for there is always forgiveness at the cross. If you are—to use the language of the prodigal son in Luke 15—in the pigsty, then admit that. Acknowledge that you need to be back home, and come humbly back God so that you can feel your Father's embrace.

If you are married, maybe you need to talk to your wife, confessing and asking her for forgiveness and support. The quality of a man's ministry is often depicted on his wife's face. Your wife doesn't need a husband who is pretending he's perfect. (Let's face it, she already knows that you're not.) Your wife does need a husband who is repenting of his sin.

Confess and find forgiveness and then kill the spider. Flee the sin. Fight the sin. Be ruthless. "If your hand causes you to stumble, cut it off. It is better for you to enter life maimed than with two hands to go into hell" (Mark 9 v 43).

So, what is in your tent? What needs bringing out into the light, for forgiveness and restoration? What is the eagle in your gut clawing its talons into you about? That's actually not an eagle. It's the Holy Spirit, and he convicts us so that we can be restored and so that we can move forward with a ministry that is underpinned by honesty and obedience. What is in your tent? Remember Achan. Take Jesus' warnings to the churches in Revelation seriously. Deal with it now. The devil's greatest lies at these moments are "No need to repent today" and "No hope for you if you do repent today". Don't try to bluff God. Sin needs to be confessed, and sin needs to be forgiven, and sin must be fought. Come to Jesus for a fresh start.

✝ ✝ ✝ ✝ ✝ ✝ ✝ ✝ ✝

CHAPTER 3

LEAD YOURSELF

✛ ✛ ✛ ✛ ✛ ✛ ✛ ✛ ✛

You cannot lead others well if you cannot lead yourself well.

A few years ago I was giving a series of evangelistic talks at Eton College, the elite (read: expensive) boarding school that has provided 20 of the UK's 55 Prime Ministers. One lunchtime I was sitting at a table opposite a 13-year-old. As we chatted, I asked him, "What is it about Eton and leadership—how do they teach you guys to be leaders?"

He shoved in a potato and thought for a moment, and then he said:

> *"Well, I've only been here for a term and a half. But I can tell you what I think: I've already found that if I don't do what I have to do, when I have to do it, I just fall behind, and then I'm struggling.*

> *"So I guess I'm learning to lead myself. And I suppose that once I learn to do that, I'll be able to lead other people."*

I think that 13-year-old had grasped what took me decades of life to work out (which is presumably why I never became Prime Minister), and what so many church leaders have never learned—perhaps because none of us have ever really talked much about it. The art of self-leadership is fundamental to successful leadership of any organisation, including (and perhaps especially) the house of God. Paul says an elder "must manage his own family well [because] if anyone does not know how to manage his own family, how can he take care of God's church?" (1 Timothy 3 v 4-5). Of course that's true—and we need to go a step further than even that, for we will never manage our biological family or our church family well if we cannot manage ourselves.

Put it another way: find a failure of pastoral leadership and, if you look underneath, you'll see a failure of self-leadership. So in this chapter, I want to lay out a framework for self-leadership that I'm seeking to live by. I'm dyslexic, so I operate through diagrams rather than lists. Here's the framework:

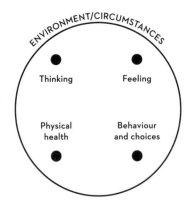

MY PERSONAL CATECHISM

I need to get my thinking right each day from the word go (or, in my case, the words "Do I really have to get up?"). In Paul's words, if I am to offer myself as a living sacrifice each day, holy and pleasing to God, then I will need to "be transformed by the renewing of [my] mind (Romans 12 v 1-2). After all, it's the "knowledge of the truth that leads to godliness" (Titus 1 v 1). So I'm very intentional first thing in the morning about getting my thinking in place. I read my Bible before I look at my technology. When I was first in ministry someone said to me that the first hour of the day is the rudder for the rest of it. So in my quiet time, I work through my own mini-catechism:

Q: Rico, when did God choose you?
A: Before the creation of the world. He chose *you* in him before the creation of the world to be holy and blameless in his sight. And he predestined *you* for adoption to sonship through Jesus Christ (Ephesians 1 v 4-5).

Q: Rico, how does God feel about you?
A: He is delighted with you because he is delighted with Jesus his Son, and you are united to Jesus by faith. A righteousness from God has been revealed, and it has been given to you (Romans 3 v 21-22). You are a sinner, and you are justified. Rico, say today what Gresham Machen said on his deathbed: "I thank God for the obedience of Jesus". Your identity is in Christ, and whether others accept you or reject you

today does not make you any more or less valuable or accepted or loved.

Q: Rico, why is today a great day?
A: Because today is the day that God has planned for you, and if God says it's good, then it's good. Whatever God brings into your day—the things you'd choose and the things you definitely wouldn't—he will work in them for your good. And your good is to become more like Jesus (Romans 8 v 28-29). So today, one way or another, whether you see it or not, you're going to grow to be more like your Saviour. That's a great day.

Q: Rico, why is today a better day than yesterday?
A: Because you're a day's march closer to home—24 hours closer to seeing Jesus face to face. You never need lose heart because though today may be hard, your troubles are the path to the eternal glory that far outweighs them all (2 Corinthians 4 v 17). What you can see is not all there is, and it will not last; what you cannot see is eternal, and you're getting closer to the day that faith becomes sight (v 18). "No human mind has conceived [of] the things God has prepared for those who love him" (1 Corinthians 2 v 9).

These things are true. They need to be at the forefront of my thoughts. This is who I am, and this is the day I'm entering. And with those in place, I'm ready to serve. And my feelings will follow my thoughts as I reflect on the wonder of the gospel.

TWO KEY FEELINGS

There are two feelings that I'm particularly concerned about and on the look-out for in myself; thanksgiving and resentment. Don't forget what resentment did to Eve: the devil convinced her that God did not want her best, and was not giving her his best. *Look at this fruit,* he said. *Of course you can take it. Of course you should have it. If God really loved you, you would be allowed it.* And she looked at the fruit, and she loved the look of it, and the independence and self-glorification it represented became an idol to her; so she took the fruit and rebelled against her loving Maker.

In the same way, resentment is where the devil really gets a grip on us. How easy it is to resent another's ministry or marriage: to resent having to disciple this church family, to serve these sinners in this place; to resent the daily sacrifices of ministry when those around us who don't even know or respect God get easy, comfortable, wealthy, healthy lives. Resentment is the child of envy, and envy is how idolatry feels. How easy it is to echo Asaph's words: "This is what the wicked are like—always free of care, they go on amassing wealth. Surely in vain I have kept my heart pure and have washed my hands in innocence" (Psalm 73 v 12-13).

The cure for resentment is thanksgiving. It's hard to feel bitter when you're at the foot of the cross, where the Son of God gave his life for you in obedience to the Father's eternal plan to save you, so that the Spirit could apply to you the benefits of Christ's sacrifice when he called you to faith in him. Lindsay Brown, who served as head of IFES, was once asked how people keep going for decades in Christian service, and he answered, "They believe two things about the gospel: that it is both true and wonderful". If we know the gospel is true but forget how wonderful it is, resentment has room to grow. By contrast, if we remember that it is both these things, thankfulness will be our dominant feeling and the driver for our ministry.

When I was a child we lived in Africa, and there was no kids TV and not many toyshops around. When my father came back from a business trip, he'd always bring me an Asterix or Tintin comic book. And I would grab it and take myself off and devour it, and, for the time it took me to read it, I was absolutely content. It was my treasure. I could have been reading it sitting on a manure heap and I would have been happy.

Is the gospel your treasure? Or has the wonder of the gospel started to slip for you? You preach it Sunday by Sunday, but has the sheer wonder of it started to fade?

You will treasure the gospel to the degree that you remember its truths and to the degree that you see your sin. Charles Simeon, the great nineteenth-century preacher who pastored in Cambridge, UK, talked about "growing downwards". If I am to be a thankful man, then I must be willing to see my sin for, when I consider my sin and then hold up God's grace, I simply cannot believe his goodness in forgiving me. And so the more we know we've been forgiven, the more we'll love the Lord (Luke 7 v 47). And the emotional marker of knowing you're a forgiven sinner is joy: the joy of gratitude. When I see both my sin and the gospel clearly, the joy of the Lord really is my strength (Nehemiah 8 v 10), and I'm ready to serve, not because I have to but because I get to.

That's the cycle: sin, grace, joy, service. You can't short-circuit that without getting into problems. When we just get up and try to go and serve our church, very quickly we'll head down into resentment—and when we function from resentment, we'll soon rebel. So get the gospel—not just its truth but its wonder—in place in your thoughts so that it can drive your feelings.

That isn't easy, for two reasons. First, because of our circumstances, which we'll come to later. But second, because most—perhaps all—of us have deeply-rooted feelings that have grown in non-gospel sediment that was laid down at formative stages of our lives. For me, because of the types of schools I went to and because I wasn't saved until my teen years, I had drilled into me that three things were true. First, you're not good enough. Second, prove yourself. Third, it's a dangerous world. And I have to remember that this is my default view of myself and the world around me, and I need to counter them with the gospel:

> *"Rico, you've been told you're not good enough; and that's true, but it's also ok, because Christ knew that and still he died for you. Your value in his eyes does not lie in your goodness or lack of it."*

> *"Rico, you were told to prove yourself; but you don't need to, because Jesus has given you his*

> *righteousness. You don't need to use your work today to prove that you're worthy of his love; you're working for him because he already loves you."*

> *"Rico, it's a dangerous world; well, yes, but the God who is sovereign over every single aspect of it is your Father, and he will bring you through and take you home."*

All that is about getting grace so firmly in place that my feelings flow from knowing I'm a sinner saved by grace to be a child of God rather than a spiritual orphan who needs to prove himself in a dangerous world.

Over the years, I have learned to kneel by my bed every morning and every night and simply give thanks, mainly for the gospel and then for the daily blessings I've seen. I learned to do that from an Australian evangelist, John Chapman, who had a huge effect on my ministry. I saw him in London once about 20 years ago. We met up for a coffee, and for about 20 minutes I took him through four or five things in my ministry that were getting me down, that were hard, that were holding back the ministry… and gradually his Australian lip curled a little in disdain at this whingeing Englishman, and he said to me, "Rico, mate, I had a friend like you, a clergyman like you, and he committed suicide. And if I may say, you're not unlike him."

I answered in the only possible way: "What?!"

He said, "Rico, there's no thanksgiving in your life. Morning and night, I want you to kneel by your bed and give thanks to God—and why don't you begin each time with the cross?"

And so I have, ever since. It has grown my thankfulness, it has throttled my resentment, and I dare say it has saved my ministry and possibly, according to John Chapman, my life.

MAKING CHOICES

Having our thoughts transformed by the gospel and our feelings driven by the gospel, we're then able to make good choices. And the most important choices are the ones where we are faced with the choice to obey or to rebel: to please our loving Father or to sin against him. What are your besetting sins? Be consciously monitoring yourself so that you can spot patterns of sin—areas of weakness. Can you name your three greatest struggles at the moment? If you can't, you're either being defeated by them or you're in glory (in which case, you're unlikely to be reading this book). So name the areas where you are regularly choosing to rebel. (If you need help, I would guess your spouse or a close friend would be able to help…)

I'm a fairly average guy, so the three areas I'm battling with constantly are anger, lust and speech. And I must fight. As John Owen put it memorably, "Be killing your sin, or it will be killing you." I must not be Achan. Here's how I'm trying to fight.

First, anger. I need to remind myself what the Scriptures say. Here are my three go-to verses on anger right now:

"A man without self-control is like a city broken into and left without walls."

(Proverbs 25 v 28, ESV)

"Anyone who is angry with a brother or sister will be subject to judgment." (Matthew 5 v 22)

"'In your anger do not sin'; do not let the sun go down while you are still angry, and do not give the devil a foothold." (Ephesians 4 v 26-27)

That last one reminds me that there is a malignant being who is out to destroy me—and my sin will give him a foothold. Gospel ministry is the frontline of a spiritual battle, and you and I are in the line. All of us have certain areas where the devil knows we're weak— whether it's anger and lust, or entitlement, self-pity, bitterness, and so on—and that's where he'll probe, in the hope that he can dismantle us and take us out of gospel ministry. But those areas of weakness are also the ones where we can take our stand, knowing that if we resist the devil, he will flee (James 4 v 7).

So I've got to remember that my enemy is real, that my anger is sinful, and that sin is radioactive. I'm a Bible teacher; I simply can't afford to be losing my temper. I've got to control it. So I have a process I work through, which I call AAR: Acknowledge, Absorb, Respond. I get cross easily. And I need to spot that it's happening. I'll be talking with someone, and they say something, and I sense the feeling rising in me, and I need to think to myself, "I'm feeling angry here. The feeling is rising. Right now, I want to take this person outside and sort this out man to man." That's what I'm thinking as I'm smiling at them. And if I don't acknowledge the feeling, I won't be in a position to control it.

Once I recognise that the anger is rising up, I can move to the second step: absorb. I do not react for 24 hours. That's my rule. I step back. I know that when the anger has risen up, I'm not in a good place to know what a wise response is, and what I feel a legitimate response would be is almost certainly not a good idea. So I absorb whatever it is that's happened or been said, and I wait 24 hours.

Then third, after 24 hours I respond. If I don't—if I just bottle it up—then eventually I will explode, probably at another person in another context. So I do need to respond, and after 24 hours I am going to be calm enough to respond wisely. Sometimes, the right response is to realise that I had no grounds for annoyance, let alone anger, and I just need to get over it and leave it. Or I'm able to consider what that person is going through and see that I simply need to forgive them and move on. Other times, responding well means going back to the person and talking it through. AAR isn't necessarily going to mean that the war with anger is finished—I guess I'll struggle with this for the rest of my earthly life. But it does mean I'm more likely to win the battle each day.

Second, lust. Having been single until I was 42, here are the verses I actively reminded myself of—and still do—to avoid kidding myself that lust doesn't really matter:

> *"I say to you that everyone who looks at a woman*
> *with lustful intent has already committed*
> *adultery with her in his heart."*
>
> *(Matthew 5 v 28, ESV)*

> *"Do you not know that your bodies are temples of*
> *the Holy Spirit, who is in you, whom you have*
> *received from God? You are not your own; you*
> *were bought at a price. Therefore honour God*
> *with your bodies." (1 Corinthians 6 v 19-20)*

> *"Treat ... younger women as sisters, with absolute*
> *purity." (1 Timothy 5 v 1-2)*

And what I need to do then is pray. Dietrich Bonhoeffer was right when he said that a praying man can't lust, and a lusting man can't pray. So I pray!

Not only that, but I make sure I am making it as hard as I can for myself to fail in this area. Part of that is simply to be busy doing gospel work. When we're genuinely engaged in the Lord's business and that is our focus, we're less likely to fall—just as if King David had been at war as he should have been, he wouldn't have had time or opportunity to gaze at Bathsheba and then call her over to the palace. But one other way that I make it hard for myself is that whenever I get a new phone or computer, I take it to a guy in my church who is a tech expert, and I get him to install things on it that will make it hard for me to watch pornography. Not to do that is like going cycling without a bike helmet on. You may be fine for a while—even for a long, long time—but eventually you will fall, and when you do, it may be catastrophic. It strikes me that most of us are fine for 97% of the time, but in the other 3% it goes wild, and we struggle to control ourselves. While I'm in the calm 97% of the time, I need to be storing up verses, praying and taking steps to keep myself pure, so that in those white-hot 3% moments, I can still guide myself.

Third, words. I have always been impetuous in my speech. When I was a young guy, I was given a verse: "Set a guard over my mouth, LORD; keep watch over the door of my lips" (Psalm 141 v 3). Decades later, I still need to pray that. I need to take seriously the command "Do not let any unwholesome talk come out of your mouths, but only what is helpful for building others up according to their needs, that it may benefit those who listen" (Ephesians 4 v 29). There is something more important than making people laugh, and certainly more important than making a good impression: building others up. The missionary Amy Carmichael famously set a threefold guard over her lips by asking herself, "Is it true? Is it helpful? Is it necessary?" I need to hear that, and I need to keep hearing that. And I need to be applying that to what I put on social media too. (Reasonably regularly I delete a comment before sending it, and not infrequently I delete something after posting it.)

Those are my struggles, and so those are the areas where I need consciously to make wise choices every day. So do you. Maybe this is a good time to put down this book again, and consider what your particular battles are, and what the right and the wrong choice will look like in each. Then identify a few verses for each that will remind you what godliness will look like, and that sin in that area is serious. Find a process that will help you fight the sin; praise God for each time you choose to honour him, and flee to the cross each time you do not. After all, only the pastor who is mortifying his own sin is able to call upon his church to mortify theirs.

REST IS NOT AN OPTIONAL EXTRA

Next on my diagram, I have physical health. If you know me (or have seen a picture of me), you'll know this area is not my strength. Someone once told me how wonderful they'd found running a marathon, and I thought about doing one myself. The next day, I had to drive 26 miles, and I thought, "You've got to be kidding! This is miles." And that was that. So this is an area that I need to be working on, and all the more so as I get older. I have a sweet tooth combined with, if I don't rein myself in, the eating habits of a teenage boy. We need to avoid making physical health an idol, but we also need to avoid ignoring our physical health altogether. Certainly where I pastor in central London, if I am not in reasonable shape, I can't expect people to want to listen to me. If we can't look after ourselves, can we expect people to trust us to look after them?

Part of watching our health is to try to get decent sleep. (Obviously if you're reading this and you have very young kids, the definition of "decent sleep" for a season may well need to be "some sleep".) Monitor your tiredness levels. An exhausted pastor is not much use to anyone, far less a pastor who's having a nervous breakdown. There have been times when I've had a particularly difficult pastoral issue to deal with, and I've got sleeping pills from the doctor so that I don't lie awake from 3 a.m. each night. There have been plenty of other times that I've just accepted that I'll probably be awake at 3 a.m. anyway, so I've made doubly sure I'm in bed on time.

And take your rest. We evangelicals are not good at this, I think. We know we are saved by grace, but then we do our ministry as though we're saved by works. If God created the cosmos in six days, then he can build the small pocket of his kingdom that you're in through six of your days each week. When he commanded his people to work six days and rest for one, he did not make an exemption for you because you're so important to his mission that he can't manage it without the extra seventh of your time. Your day off is your statement that you truly believe that the Lord is sovereign. There will always be more good things you could do, and so by taking a day off you will always be choosing not to do good things. But you have to leave the work with him. (It was always his work anyway.) Unless he builds the house, you labour in vain; and he's perfectly capable of building the house without your help.

Often we act as though rest is not really an option. And it isn't, but not in the way we think. Rest is not an option. It's a command of God, and so it's a necessity for us. A friend of mine who is an evangelist once said to me, "I missed my days off. Then I had a breakdown, and I took all the days off I'd missed in a row."

So take your day off. Set it, communicate it to your church family and stick to it. I give my phone to my wife—it's my way of saying, "I belong to the family today. Today my total priority is being a husband and a father, not a pastor or a teacher." On the (very) rare occasions that I realise that doing some admin first thing will enable me to switch off more fully for the rest of the day, I ask (not tell) her first, and we agree exactly how long I will do it for.

And on that day, do something that you love. Do something that is genuinely restful. For one guy (not me), it may be running a marathon. For another, it may be renovating a house (again, not me). We're wired differently, so we will rest differently; but rest we must.

For me, it's reading rugby autobiographies. I've got about 300. I'm not sure I told my wife about this before we married. The great thing about a rugby autobiography is that nothing much bad happens. The worst that you read about is that someone got kicked in the head or injured after a successful career. (If they weren't successful, they won't have written an autobiography.) I read *The Week* news round-up magazine (sadly, I grew up, and it replaced the comics). I watch war films. I make sure I spend some time with my wife. I take my kids swimming. I play golf once a month.

To be honest, my day off doesn't always all feel restful. Spending time with young kids is not necessarily what you would call "a rest". But afterwards, I do usually feel refreshed. And, because I've given my subconscious a bit of time off, too, I tend to find that I have my best ideas the day after my day off.

We were made to work hard, and faithfully, for six days a week. But we were also made to rest one day a week. Be unashamed about taking your day of rest and about actually resting on it.

CIRCUMSTANCES WEIGH

Finally, there's environment or circumstances. Don't underestimate the effect that a difficult church issue, or pastoral situation, or family circumstance, or relative rejecting the gospel can have on you. I've dealt with the pastoral aftermath of six suicides in the past couple of years. That's brutal. I resigned from the Archbishop's Commission on Evangelism and publicly stated my reasons why—for a while if you googled my name, interviews with me about it came up top, and organisations started withdrawing speaking invitations. That was draining and worrying. Before his death my father suffered with violent dementia for five years. He had a police escort out of one residential carehome because he was wielding knives. We had to try to calm him down and find somewhere safe for him to stay. It was my dad—it was heartbreaking; it was brutal.

And be aware of the people you have around you. I'm struck by the way in the Proverbs we are not only presented with the wise person and the fool, but also with the predators who can turn the wise foolish—most notably the adulterous woman and the bloodthirsty man. Sexual immorality will destroy your ministry, and very possibly your marriage. Constant fighting will undermine your ministry, and very possibly your health. So be aware of who you need to be careful of. They may be in your family. They may well be in your church. Set wise boundaries, even as you seek to love those on the other side of them. If you're married, if ever your spouse has concerns about others, listen to them. No one in ministry plans on having an affair or on being drawn into petty, unnecessary conflicts—but I've seen pastors be destroyed by both.

So don't underestimate the influence of your circumstances or of the people around you. We need to recognise the effect that these things can have. When our environment is difficult, our resentment levels more easily rise and our sin is more easily excused. So when my circumstances are hard in one way or another, I need to remember the gospel in that, I need to battle sin during that, and I need to take my rest during that.

JOIN THE CIA

Self-leadership is essential, but it is not easy—and so being willing to listen and willing to be held accountable is utterly key. So first, we need to be ready to learn from those who have walked this way before us. When I was a younger pastor, I and another young pastor set up a meeting called the "Rehoboam group", named after Solomon's son, who so tragically listened only to his contemporaries and never to his elders, and lost the greater part of his kingdom as a result (see 1 Kings 12 v 6-17). The idea was simple: we simply invited along someone thirty years older than us to share their wisdom, and we listened hard.

Second, as I said earlier, we need friends. Not acquaintances whom we can keep at arm's length if we're burying sin under our tent or buckling under the strain of our ministry circumstances or swerving from the straight line of teaching the word properly. Not mates who we can have a joke with but cannot pray with— who we can talk about sports with but not confide our struggles to. We need friends with whom we commit to the CIA—confidentiality, intimacy, accountability. We need friends whom we trust to ask the questions that we'd rather not answer, and to help us with our sin by refusing to help us belittle or excuse or justify it, but instead by praying with us, pointing us back to grace and checking in on us. We need friends who we know will be there when we need them, whether we realise we need them or not.

One of the great blessings of my life has been a group of five friends who I am accountable with. We speak regularly and meet up about once a year. They have permission to speak into my life. We lean on each other and learn from each other: about how to do our work and interact with our colleagues, about theology, about marriage and parenting, about responding well to what's going on in our lives. I know these men care more about my godliness than about puffing me up: that they'll say what needs to be said rather than what

I want to hear. Do you have at least one friend who is like that? Perhaps it's your spouse, and that's great. If it is, get another one (friend, that is, not spouse).

And third, and perhaps most important of all, we need to have a pastor—because every pastor needs pastoring. For years I visited a man named Dr Monty Barker with a list of things I knew I needed to talk about (my wife would help me compile it…). The man who helps me in this way now is named Glynn Harrison, who wrote *The Big Ego Trip*. In England, we've recently had a desperately sad spate of pastors who have fallen from grace, and what has emerged each time is a part of their life they had kept secret—but also it has become clear that no one was holding them accountable. Here's what Glynn says of his experience of Christian leaders:

> *"I have met so many pastors who are stuck in a lonely struggle with personal issues, or operating as secretive and sometimes deceitful mavericks. They get into trouble because they have never opened their heart to pastoral care and discipline—to somebody who is older and wiser and who won't let them pull the wool over their eyes. Friends are not necessarily the answer—most men I know have acquaintances they can subtly manage out of an uncomfortable situation rather than soul-friends who will confront or counsel them. A pastor needs to find a pastor to pastor them." (Personal Correspondence)*

In other words, CIA—confidentiality, intimacy, accountability. Somebody who you run your big decisions past. Someone who can counsel you, challenge you and help you. If only Achan had had someone like that—someone who could have asked him where he'd been in Jericho, who already knew of his struggles with envy and a desire for wealth, and who could have said to him, "Dig it up *now*. Repent of it *now*. Go and give it back *now*."

So I have someone I meet with once a month and, among others, we ask each other this question: "What question do you not want me to ask you?" He helps me to lead myself well, so that I can lead my family and the household of God well.

This is self-leadership. Every morning, I deliberately focus on my thoughts, my feelings, my choices, my health and my environment. And through the day, I'm consciously seeking to let the gospel fill my thoughts, shape my feelings and direct my choices as well as my need to rest and the effect my environment is having on me. And this matters not only for ourselves but for our ministry because, once we have learned to lead ourselves, then we will be able to lead others—to the glory of God and for the good of his church.

✝ ✝ ✝ ✝ ✝ ✝ ✝ ✝ ✝

CHAPTER 4

SERVE YOUR CHURCH

✦ ✦ ✦ ✦ ✦ ✦ ✦ ✦ ✦

When it comes to leading (whether it's a church, a family, a youth group or any other group of people), there is a daily choice between two very different value systems.

And that daily choice defines you and it defines your ministry—for we are the choices that we make.

There are many books on leadership, secular and Christian. There are many strategies and metrics and structures and self-awareness tools. There are coaches and courses and conferences. And there's a reason for that—leadership is hard; it requires thought to do well, and you never really arrive (there is only one perfect leader, and he's in heaven). In this chapter I do not want to sum up, add to, or undermine any of that. There is far more to leadership than what I am going to talk about here. But there must never be less to Christian leadership than the choice I want to major on here, for this is about the core motivation that drives the rest.

The leadership choice we each face comes in three parts, and it is exemplified on the road to Jerusalem, as Jesus walked with his disciples towards his death on a Roman cross. If the Old Testament passage that has most marked me is the one that we focused on in chapter 2 as we learned from Achan, the New Testament text that has most impacted me may well be Mark 10 v 35-45. I heard John Stott preach on it, and then watched him live it (and this chapter borrows from his preaching on this passage). This text in Mark never fails to drive me to my knees, because it confronts me with the choice that everyone in Christian leadership must make: the choice between leading like Jesus, by pursuing Jesus-like greatness, and leading like the world, by pursuing what the world defines as greatness. There is absolutely no possibility of harmonisation between these two philosophies of life.

And on that road in Mark 10, James and John represent the world's ways, as Jesus embodies the heavenly way.

SELF-SERVING OR SELF-SACRIFICE

On the road to Jerusalem, much to the disciples' confusion and incomprehension, Jesus' topic of conversation was often death—his own death:

> *"They were on their way up to Jerusalem, with Jesus leading the way, and the disciples were astonished, while those who followed were afraid. Again he took the Twelve aside and told them what was going to happen to him. 'We are going up to Jerusalem,' he said, 'and the Son of Man will be*

84

delivered over to the chief priests and the teachers
of the law. They will condemn him to death and
will hand him over to the Gentiles, who will mock
him and spit on him, flog him and kill him. Three
days later he will rise.'" (Mark 10 v 32-34)

When talk turns to death, we tend to avoid it or deflect it. The disciples tried both. But sometimes, talk of death leads us to reflect on our life. What do we want from it? What do we want to do with it and achieve in it?

James and John found themselves thinking about how to secure what they wanted out of life. And they knew who could give it to them:

"James and John, the sons of Zebedee, came to
[Jesus.] 'Teacher,' they said, 'we want you to do
for us whatever we ask.'" (v 35)

Their request triggers the famous conversation between themselves and Jesus, and then between all the disciples and Jesus, that leads to the Lord's oft-quoted words in verse 45:

"The Son of Man did not come to be served, but to
serve, and to give his life as a ransom for many."

Of course, this is a familiar passage. The question isn't really whether we know it. The question is whether we've ever applied it to our own ministry. The question is whether we live it.

Here, then, is the first choice you are confronted by on the Jerusalem road. Will your leadership be marked by self-seeking or self-sacrifice?

There's an irony in verse 35 when James and John call Jesus "Teacher", because they haven't absorbed the central facets of his teaching. No—they have imbibed a very different spirit, and they are fired by a very different ambition:

> *"Let one of us sit at your right and the other at your left in your glory."*

They want the top seats around Jesus' cabinet table when he brings his kingdom in all its power. They have anticipated that one day there will be an unholy scramble for seats in Jesus' kingdom. So they judge it prudent to get in first and make an advanced reservation, and they are determined to bend Jesus' will to their own.

Jesus, this is what I want you to do—that is their prayer. They're go-getters; they're status-seekers. They are hungry for fame and honour, and they want to win. They are people who measure life by achievement and adulation. They want fame and achievement and recognition, and they are aggressively ambitious for them. They are like the Pharisees, who stood on street corners to pray "to be seen by others" (Matthew 6 v 5). Why the corner of the street? So that twice as many people would notice and be impressed by them.

This is the way the world tends to work. And let us not be in any doubt that far too often, this is the way our churches work too. I can relate to those Pharisees: doing their ministry to be seen and respected. I want to be known and admired. I want recognition. And I will go after those things that have a capacity to deliver what I want. We are all by nature Jameses and Johns, and the world cheers us on.

But the way of the cross is utterly incompatible with self-serving.

Jesus gave his life away. Jesus did not count equality with God a prize or privilege to be selfishly enjoyed, even though, as God the Son, he had every right to. "He made himself nothing by taking the very nature of a servant, being made in human likeness ... he humbled himself by becoming obedient to death—even death on a cross!" (Philippians 2 v 7-8).

Jesus did not hang on to what was rightfully his. He did not get hung up about his rights. His incarnation was an act of self-sacrifice, exceeded only in the history of humanity by his crucifixion. He did not use his divinity as an excuse to strut around the stage of human history. No, he used his humanity in order to die a criminal's death, by his own choice. (The Greek in Philippians 2 v 7-8, "he made himself ... he humbled himself" is reflexive—meaning that he did this to himself.)

Here is Jesus' way of leadership. He chose humanity. He chose the cross. He chose to pay our ransom. He chose our interests above his own. He chose opprobrium rather than adulation, so passionate was he for the welfare of others and the glory of God.

Our models of leadership will always be challenged by his. Does our way of leading risk our reputation because it sees us mixing with dropouts and those society deems untouchable? Does our way of leading risk our wellbeing because it sees us never thinking of ourselves? Jesus presents us with a choice that we do not want to be faced by: will we live for honour, glory and prestige... or self-sacrifice? We have to choose—and we are the choices that we make.

POWER OR SERVICE

Next, the road to Jerusalem confronts us with the choice between worldly power and godly service. What were James and John expecting to sit on at the right and left of Jesus in his kingdom? They were anticipating thrones. They wanted to be enthroned on either side of him. Of course, Jesus would have the highest place in his kingdom. But imagine being his number 2! That would be some power. And that is what James and John were looking for.

James and John had left behind a successful family fishing business to follow Jesus. Their father, Zebedee, had men—very possibly servants—working for him. Presumably they had stood to inherit all that, but then they had heeded Jesus' call to follow him. It would be only human to miss some of what they had left behind—to wonder what might have been if they had taken a different path through life. But Jesus was bringing God's kingdom—so at the end of the road with him lay more power than they would ever have enjoyed on the shores of the Sea of Galilee, running the fishing business of Zebedee & Sons.

This request, then, is all about power. And again, wielding power is the way of the world. The world understands the language of power. We live in a grasping, acquisitive society that respects very little, but it does respect power.

Their power-hunger explains why they hear Jesus say, *I'll be spat at, flogged and killed,* and they ignore all that and think, *What can you do for me? How can I get what I want from you?* That's how power-hungry people act. Others are there to help us up the ladder, or they are there to be kicked off the ladder. The power mindset does not see outside its own vision. It cannot. It does what it likes, when it likes, to whom it likes. It's not committed to the wellbeing of others. It's after control, influence and domination. And it won't stop to listen.

Many of us will have experienced that sort of approach to life in business or industry. And the church is not inoculated against a leadership that is all about power. The power mindset is what leads to the bullying or controlling behaviour that is, tragically, far too often seen in evangelicalism when church leaders functionally view their leadership of their church as a benign (or not so benign) dictatorship. It is what leads to pastors seeing obedience to them as identical to obedience to the gospel; it is what prompts pastors to adopt a "my way is God's way—so get on board or get out" mentality. The pulpit can so easily be turned into a throne, from where power is used to control and coerce.

But the way of the cross is utterly incompatible with that kind of power-hunger.

Jesus called together his followers (who were indignant with James and John, presumably because the brothers had got their request in before they could) for a lesson on leadership. We'd do well to listen to it, every day of our ministry.

The way of the world, Jesus says, is to use power and position to "lord it over" others—to "exercise authority over" others for the sake of the one who has authority. And then come four words that must change and shape us if we would be Christ-like leaders:

"Not so with you."

Why? Because:

"Whoever wants to become great among you must be your servant, and whoever wants to be first must be slave of all." (Mark 10 v 43)

Those words make it crystal clear that the Christian community is to operate on an entirely different principle to the secular community around us. There is no harmonisation here. If we want to seek true greatness, then it is expressed in service. The word translated "servant" is *diakonos*: one whose activities are not directed by their own interests but by the interests of another. True greatness shows itself in humble service.

I remember attending a conference a while ago that had brought together 10,000 evangelists. An older pastor I knew had been asked to give a fifteen-minute talk at the end of the final meeting, and I knew he had worked extremely hard on every line of his address. But that morning, the music band went so far beyond their allotted time that he was left with just two minutes to give his talk.

I found him backstage straight afterwards. I was livid. He was humble: "We're just servants, Rico," he said to me. That was a gospel minister who truly saw his role as being about service, and who saw that serving role as a privilege. Here was a man who got more godly, not less, under pressure.

"Whoever wants to be first must be slave of all." It is that simple and it is that challenging. Kingdom leadership looks like slavery. A slave, of course, belongs to others. I am a slave of Jesus Christ, and I belong to him and to his people. This is an utterly different approach to leadership. Those under the pastor's authority are not there for him; he is there for them. Christian leadership is exercised by example and not by coercion. If you tell people what to do more than you show them what to do, that is not Christ-like leadership. There must be no trampling in the Christian church.

One crucial implication of this for our times right now is that leaders should listen more than they speak. Neither James and John nor the Pharisees were willing to listen because listening is costly: it takes time, it may mean that we hear things we do not want to, and it is always so much easier just to tell people to come to heel than to make the effort to hear them and perhaps learn from them. Faithful leaders listen well—and I know that in my particular part of evangelicalism in my particular part of the world, this has simply not happened.

Too often, leaders have been harsh or arrogant or distant in their leadership. We haven't been willing to listen to criticism and we haven't been willing to listen to concerns, and that has caused immeasurable pain to God's people and damage to our witness. We have sent away those who told us what we did not like to hear. We have dismissed those who were not in our theological "tribe" even though they had important things to say. And in light of all that, to start to listen will take more effort than we might realise. It will require being proactive: inviting those who we know are critical of us to have a conversation with us, in which we work hard to understand them and see if and (probably) where we need to change. We might not agree with everything that they say, but we need to be humble and ready to listen and change. Those who are very different from us can expose our casual assumptions and our complete blindspots. Those who are not our friends may well find it easier to speak truth to us, for they have less to lose if we respond badly. Never assume you know enough about someone or something or a particular situation without listening, and listening hard, first.

Christian leaders are called to be servants, not bosses. We could do worse than have those four words written on our study desks, in our calendars and in our pulpits:

"Not so with you."

After all, we follow a King who came to serve. The One through whom all things were created did not come to sit on a throne the weight of which would be borne by the service of others. No—he came to carry a cross of shame, to bear the weight of others. T.W. Manson, the New Testament scholar, wrote:

> *"In the kingdom of God, service is not a stepping stone to nobility. It is nobility, the only nobility that is recognised." (The Church's Ministry, page 27)*

Service is the only nobility that is recognized. Here is the great nineteenth century bishop, J.C. Ryle:

> *"The greatest clergyman in the church is he who is most conformed to the example of Christ by humility, love and continued attendance on his flock and one who looks on himself as a servant of the children of God."*

So the symbol of authentic Christian leadership is none of the trappings of clerical success, be they a purple shirt, a perfectly crafted PR photo, a large house or a huge Twitter following. It is the towel of the Lord Jesus Christ, who washed his followers' feet even as he drew close to his own death.

That is a challenge. But it is also a great encouragement. To the world, a ministry that is centred on such service looks very ordinary. But in the eyes of the King who washed his subjects' feet, it carries nobility. We need to remember this, because most of us will only even be ordinary. D.A. Carson points this out in his book *Memoirs of an Ordinary Pastor*, which focuses on the ministry of his father, a pastor in French-speaking Canada:

> *"Most pastors will not regularly preach to thousands,
> let alone tens of thousands … They will plug away
> at their care for the aged, and their visitation,
> at their counselling, at their Bible studies and
> preaching … Once in a while they will cast a
> wistful eye on 'successful' ministries. Many of them
> will attend the conferences sponsored by the revered
> masters and come away with a slightly discordant
> combination of, on the one hand, gratitude and
> encouragement, and, on the other, jealousy, feelings
> of inadequacy, and guilt. Most of us—let us be
> frank—are ordinary pastors."*
>
> *(Kindle Location 113)*

We need to embrace the ordinariness of much of our calling—because our calling is to serve, not to be seen. And after all, it is in fact all seen by the only eyes that matter, and in his sight no act of service for Jesus' cause is truly "ordinary".

Again, Jesus presents us with a choice that often we do not want to be faced by. There is no middle way, for we claim to follow a King whose throne was a cross and whose crown was made from thorns. Will we be hungry for power or hungry to serve? We have to choose—and we are the choices that we make.

SECURITY OR SUFFERING

Third, in Christian leadership we have to choose between security and suffering.

James and John didn't know what they were asking Jesus (v 38). "Can you," asks Christ, "drink the cup

94

I drink?" James and John, their gaze filled with what they thought they could gain from following Jesus, presumably thought of the cup of wine that they would be drinking at the messianic banquet. *Of course we can drink it*, they replied. But Jesus was seeking to divert their eyes to see what they would give up in following him. The cup he was to drink was the cup of suffering for his people, the cup he resolved to drink in Gethsemane, the cup he drank to its dregs at Calvary.

And so what Jesus promises these two men is very striking, and sobering: "You will drink the cup I drink". These two men would, in time, discover what Christian leadership really involves. It means suffering—to follow a King rejected by this world means to also be rejected by this world. James was the first apostolic martyr, put to death by King Herod (Acts 12 v 2). John suffered exile on Patmos, far from church family, having endured decades of suffering and watching his co-workers be killed and the churches face persecution. That was the cup they would drink. One martyred, one enduring, both suffering. Neither was able to live a quiet, undemanding life surrounded by possessions and enjoying a respected position. Their father's fishing business could have provided them with that. Jesus' business did not.

The world seeks position to provide security: the pension, the house, the money in the bank, the college fund. We work hard so that we can control tomorrow.

But the way of the cross is utterly incompatible with that kind of chasing of security.

To follow Jesus is to leave our worldly security behind, to give up looking for it ahead, and to simply follow where he leads. And that must be more, not less, the case for those in gospel leadership than it is for those in gospel fellowships. How easy it is for us to call our people to make decisions that lead to their career suffering, their wealth suffering or their friendships suffering—and then not be willing to do so ourselves. How easy it is for us to feel entitled to the level of security that our culture says we need rather than accept the suffering that our Lord says we must walk through.

John Stott has written on these verses:

> *"Where is the spirit of adventure, the sense of uncalculating solidarity with the underprivileged? Where are the Christians who are prepared to put service before security, compassion before comfort, hardship before ease? Thousands of pioneer Christian tasks are waiting to be done, which challenge our complacency, and which call for risk. Insistence on security is incompatible with the way of the cross."*
>
> *(The Cross of Christ, page 333)*

"Safety first" can never be a pastor's motto, for we follow a Saviour who quite deliberately and resolutely stepped out of safety and into danger: who swapped the security of heaven for the suffering of a cross. To follow him is to choose to embrace suffering and eschew security, even as the world does exactly the opposite. And we are the choices that we make.

JOYFUL LEADERSHIP

Self-sacrifice... service... suffering. These are all part of Christian leadership, because this is Christ-like leadership. And so in verse 45 lies the power to live joyfully by a set of leadership values that are utterly incomprehensible to the world:

> *"Even the Son of Man did not come to be served, but to serve, and to give his life as a ransom for many." (Mark 10 v 45)*

When you lead by serving, you get to *be like* Jesus. Ministry is a daily opportunity to be conformed into the image of God's Son (Romans 8 v 29). There is something deeply attractive about seeing someone who is genuinely, authentically putting others' interests before their own. It's one of the things that makes Jesus so beautiful, isn't it? We follow the most powerful man in the universe, who used all that power to serve. On a microcosmic level the pastor has the opportunity to do likewise, every day, in many ways. So we do not live this way because we have to so much as because we get to—we get to be like Christ.

As the writer and elder Jonathan Leeman puts it, this means that the Christian in a place of authority or influence will...

> *"use your leadership position to do what Jesus said: don't look to be served but to serve. This doesn't mean you don't lead. Jesus led. It means not clinching your leadership with a tight fist. Instead, you're always preparing to give it away,*

*to it let go, even to the point of your death. You
know God will raise you up in due time, and
so in the meantime you give yourself entirely to
raising [those you are ministering to] up—to be
your equal, or even your better."*

*(9marks.org/article/fighting-the-temptations-of-
successful-leadership, accessed June 24th 2020)*

Second, when you lead by serving, you get to *please*
Jesus. As we offer ourselves in his service, we please
God (Romans 12 v 1). Of course, this is the case for
every believer—but in one sense those in full-time
ministry are in the wonderful position of having
more opportunities to live it. A wise older pastor said
to me as I started out that I must make sure I always
did things for the gospel. If you do things primarily
for yourself, you're twisting Christian ministry into
self-serving self-promotion. If you do things primarily
for your church, you'll grow jaded, cynical or bitter
because your church will let you down. But do things
for the Jesus who never has and never will let you
down and you will be ready to serve, in whatever way
you're called to. In this sense there'll be no difference
between bathing your child and giving a talk at a huge
conference. Both will be about serving. And so serving
to please Jesus proves to be a far more satisfying way
to live than spending our time labouring to build our
own empires:

*"It is a wonderfully liberating experience when the
desire to please God overtakes the desire to please*

ourselves, and when love for others displaces love for self. True freedom is not freedom from responsibility to God and others in order to live for ourselves, but freedom from ourselves in order to live for God and others."
(Stott, 1&2 Thessalonians, page 91)

Third, in leading in this way, you get to *display* Jesus. When I think of the men I have wanted to follow, and whom, as I look back, I am still glad that I followed, their supreme quality was not their charisma or their preaching or their vision or their humour; it was their servant-heartedness. If you want people to follow you, to keep following you, and to be glad years later that they chose to follow you, then show them Christ in the way you lead them. Let them see you washing feet. Let them see you serving rather than being served. That is compelling. Sometimes when I speak of Jesus calling Christians to give up their lives and follow him, I say, "Of course, Jesus carried his own cross. He isn't asking you to do anything he isn't prepared to do himself." That is the Lord's point in verse 45 here: *your greatness must be expressed in service*, he tells the first pastors of the Christian church, *because you follow a God who is greater than you can imagine, and who stooped lower to serve than you can grasp.*

During the Covid-19 lockdown of spring 2020, the Chief Medical Officer of Scotland, Dr Catherine Calderwood, told everyone to stay home and not leave their houses except for essential travel—and then she was revealed to have been driving between her town house and her second home every weekend. A month or so later, Neil Ferguson, the British epidemiologist whose projections had guided much of the government's response to the virus, was caught ignoring the lockdown to visit his lover in her home. And just weeks after that, the Prime Minister's right-hand man, Dominic Cummings, was found to have broken the lockdown rules too. (I had to keep rewriting this paragraph as the examples mounted up.) For all three of them, in the space of a single news item their right to call people to make sacrifices and serve others evaporated. So it is with us. If there is a gap between what we preach and teach to others and practice ourselves, it can be hidden for a while but not for very long. So as I look at my own ministry, I need to ask myself this uncomfortable question: as I ask others to sacrifice, to serve, to suffer, can I honestly say (as Jesus could) that I'm not asking them to do anything that I'm not doing or prepared to do myself?

Inauthenticity is corrosive. But an authentic ministry is precious. We get to show people Christ by living and leading like Christ.

THE YARDSTICK

This is the attitude of successful ministry. It is the pattern we find written throughout Paul's letters. To take just one example, here he is speaking to the church in Colossae. Read these words as those of a man who knew what it meant to follow the King who came to serve and to give his life as a ransom for many:

"I rejoice in what I am suffering for you, and I fill up in my flesh what is still lacking in regard to Christ's afflictions, for the sake of his body, which is the church. I have become its servant by the commission God gave me to present to you the word of God in its fullness— the mystery that has been kept hidden for ages and generations, but is now disclosed to the Lord's people. To them God has chosen to make known among the Gentiles the glorious riches of this mystery, which is Christ in you, the hope of glory. He is the one we proclaim, admonishing and teaching everyone with all wisdom, so that we may present everyone fully mature in Christ. To this end I strenuously contend with all the energy Christ so powerfully works in me."   *(Colossians 1 v 24-29)*

Here is the ultimate yardstick of our leadership:

- I am willing, and happy, to suffer for the good of you whom God has given me to serve.
- I am presenting the word of God in its fullness to you.
- I am proclaiming Christ—and that means teaching and warning you as wisely as I can.
- My overriding aim is to help you to become more like Jesus.
- I am working as hard as I can, with all the energy I've been given.

And the question is, Can we say the same thing to our own churches?

The answer, of course, is something like this: *Sometimes. A bit. At times, more. At times, much less.* And so we must come back to Mark 10 v 45, and remember that even as pastors—especially as pastors—we are not saved by following Jesus' example but by trusting in his sacrifice. He came to "give his life as a ransom for many", and the "many" includes us. We get it wrong. We lead in ways that are self-seeking, hungry for power, or aiming for security. And when we do, there is forgiveness. And because we're forgiven, we can keep going, and keep growing, and keep leading our Lord's sheep. We don't minister in order to gain God's approval but because we have it. It is knowing that you are ransomed by Christ that means you will keep enjoying getting to serve like Christ, become like Christ, please Christ, and show more of Christ.

THE LEAST IMPORTANT

Our attitude towards leadership will always show itself in the way we treat those who can do little for us. The colleague of a friend of mine puts it concisely and very challengingly: "You can tell a great deal about a man by whether he notices and how he speaks to the least important person in a room".

We can tell a great deal about those men on the road to Jerusalem in how they treated the least important. We see the disciples arguing about who was the greatest (Mark 9 v 34); we see Jesus marching towards serving them in his death (v 31). And we see those disciples giving no time to children, and the Lord

Jesus making the time to take them in his arms and bless them.

Small children, in some measure today but to a far greater extent in that society, could give you nothing: no status, no affirmation, no security. They could only take and never give. That is why the disciples had no time for them, and that is why Jesus made time for them. The way the disciples saw their ministry was seen in how they saw those children.

After I left university, I served on staff at one of England's largest, most prominent Anglican churches. The minister was called Paul Berg. He ran a large staff team, was respected by pastors throughout the country, and (in an age before podcasts) spoke regularly to many hundreds and had influence over many thousands. When he retired, he moved to a small village in the countryside. After he died, his wife told me that the church in that village had wanted to hold a Bible-study group for young mothers, but could not start it because there was no one to look after the toddlers.

So Paul looked after them.

When his wife told me that story, I wasn't surprised, because I'd known Paul. And that was who he was. That kind of story fitted right in with the man I'd known. Paul followed a divine servant who had stooped lower than he could imagine, and so Paul joyfully stooped to serve too.

That's Christian leadership. That's the mark of greatness. Not how he spoke at conferences but in how he volunteered to serve in a kids' group. That's a man who has heard, "Well done, good and faithful servant" from the lips of the one he'd lived for and whose example he had followed and displayed.

James and John wanted to be in the cabinet, and Jesus told them that they must go into the kindergarten. So must we. Those who are the rulers of this world lord it over others and exercise their authority for their own sake, power and security. Not so with you. For even the Son of Man did not come to be served, but to serve, and to give his life as a ransom for many. Instead, whoever wants to become great must be a servant—a servant who knows that success is being faithful in the things that really matter, and so who defines success biblically, fights their sin ruthlessly, leads themselves carefully, and serves their church wholeheartedly.

+ + + + + + + + +

Afterword

✦ ✦ ✦ ✦ ✦ ✦ ✦ ✦ ✦

Listening is so much easier among friends—particularly within our own social or religious cohort, where we feel safe and supported. But recent events in the church have raised serious questions about how we listen and whom we listen to, and the impact of those choices upon the life of the church.

In the UK, the Independent Inquiry into Child Sexual Abuse (IICSA) has scrutinised the way Anglican and Roman Catholic churches have handled historic allegations of abuse. Several reports have contained horrifying examples of clergy-perpetrated abuse, matched only by the appalling failure of Christian leaders to listen to those who were abused. The US, Australia and the rest of the world have seen their own, similar, scandals.

In the UK there are several inquiries currently underway. These reports are focussed on a group of evangelical leaders who fell far short of the trust put in them. Some of the abuse was associated with the summer camps that took place at Iwerne Minster in Dorset.

I went to Iwerne, twice as a camper and then, after a four-year gap, as a room leader, volunteering over several summers from the late 1980s into the early 90s. Although I did not know any of the victims, I have since read their stories with revulsion and grief at what they went through. As we (at the point of writing this) await the findings of the respective inquiries, we must commit ourselves to listening to the survivors of abuse, and taking any further action to ensure that justice is served.

In his book *The Social Sources of Denominationalism*, Richard Niebuhr argues that denominationalism is not primarily a theological but a social phenomenon. That is, our tendency is to stick with those in our social constituency and pay little attention to those on the outside. But the cost of doing this has been the very credibility of our Christian witness.

The failure to listen and respond wasn't simply a fundamental failure of leadership; it allowed the continuation of criminal conduct and the ongoing exploitation and abuse of victims, and it has led to the justifiable condemnation of Christianity in Britain by investigating bodies and the public more generally. The price of not listening could not have been higher. Though it may challenge our pride, and cost us our comfortable assumptions and even some friends, if we are to be faithful leaders then we must be quick to listen, and we must repent individually and call for wider repentance where necessary. We will only do this if we care more for God's verdict and for those who are hurting and vulnerable than we do about the opinions of those in our ministry or social circles.

February 2021

QUESTIONS FOR REFLECTION
OR DISCUSSION

These questions are intended for you to think about, and ideally to talk through with someone else, so that what you've read in this book might shape your ministry as the Spirit guides and equips you.

CHAPTER ONE: DEFINE SUCCESS

- What things am I tempted to see as indicators of success? What impact does this have (or could this have, over the long term) on my ministry, my relationships and my health?
- Do I consistently do my best to handle the word of truth correctly—making my teaching both faithful and clear? What could I do to work harder on this?
- What temptations are there for me to swerve from the truth? What are the specific dangers for the people I minister to, if I give in to those temptations?
- Do I have people to run my teaching past before I give it, for both faithfulness and relevance—a small group that comprises men and women, old and young, and is racially diverse?
- What ungodly desires do I need to start or keep fleeing from? When am I tempted to be unkind or uncontrolled in my speech?

CHAPTER TWO: FIGHT YOUR SIN

- What is my attitude towards sin, generally? Do I take it as seriously as God takes it? When I speak about it, what do I say?
- When am I tempted to keep my sin a secret? What impact does that have on those I serve?
- How often do I repent of my own sins? What am I doing to lead others in repentance?
- When I am leading a ministry or mission initiative, do I make sure that confession and repentance are part of the preparation for every Christian involved?
- Am I ever too tolerant of sins among the people I lead? Conversely, am I ever too harsh in the way I deal with others' sin?

CHAPTER THREE: LEAD YOURSELF

- How often do I remind myself of the sheer wonder of the gospel? Do I need to change my spiritual routines to ensure that it happens?
- What impact has my past had on what drives me, and on the way I view the world? How does the gospel speak into that?
- Am I taking my day of rest and actually resting on it? What needs to change?
- Do I have a small group who I can walk through life with and be accountable to? If not, what steps could I take towards having that?

- Does someone ask me each month, "What question do you not want me to ask you?" If not, who will I ask?
- Do I have a pastor's pastor—someone older and wiser than me, whose wisdom can't be bluffed?

CHAPTER FOUR: SERVE YOUR CHURCH

- What aspect of worldly "greatness" do I most desire—prestige, money, security, influence? How can I flee from that desire?
- Is there any part of leadership that I need to approach differently (or even lay down for a while) in order to cultivate a more servant-hearted attitude?
- How well am I listening? Am I actively inviting those who I know have a different perspective from me, or even would be critical of me, to come and share their insights and concerns with me?
- Who do I find it hardest to serve? Am I setting them a good example? How will I love them well?
- What aspect of earthly security am I most afraid of losing, and how might that affect my decisions and priorities in ministry? What am I doing to prepare myself to suffer and still rejoice?
- How does my ministry match up to the yardstick of Colossians 1? In which ways do I

need to return to Jesus, and ask his Spirit to change me to make me more like him?
- In what way am I intentionally developing people around me, and supportively delegating roles and responsibilities to them?

- In what three ways do I most want this book to reshape my approach to my ministry? What practical steps do I need to take? Whose help do I need to enlist?
- What has this book shown me of Jesus that has caused me to be more in love with him, and more excited to serve him?

thegoodbook

COMPANY

BIBLICAL | RELEVANT | ACCESSIBLE

At The Good Book Company, we are dedicated to helping Christians and local churches grow. We believe that God's growth process always starts with hearing clearly what he has said to us through his timeless word—the Bible.

Ever since we opened our doors in 1991, we have been striving to produce Bible-based resources that bring glory to God. We have grown to become an international provider of user-friendly resources to the Christian community, with believers of all backgrounds and denominations using our books, Bible studies, devotionals, evangelistic resources, and DVD-based courses.

We want to equip ordinary Christians to live for Christ day by day, and churches to grow in their knowledge of God, their love for one another, and the effectiveness of their outreach.

Call us for a discussion of your needs or visit one of our local websites for more information on the resources and services we provide.

Your friends at The Good Book Company

thegoodbook.com | thegoodbook.co.uk
thegoodbook.com.au | thegoodbook.co.nz
thegoodbook.co.in